Contents

KU-130-215

Preface

The Key Facts series is a practical and complete revision aid that can be used by students of law courses at all levels from A Level to degree and beyond, and in professional and vocational courses.

The Key Facts series is designed to give a clear view of each subject. This will be useful to students when tackling new topics and is invaluable as a revision aid. Most chapters open with an outline in diagram form of the points covered in that chapter. The points are then developed in a structured list form to make learning easier. Supporting cases are given throughout by name and for some complex areas facts are given to reinforce the point being made.

The Key Facts series aims to accommodate the syllabus content of most qualifications in a subject area, using many visual learning aids.

EU Law is now a core subject in all qualifying law degrees. It is also a vital subject in which to gain a good understanding since so many other areas of law now are affected by it. It would be difficult to teach or study, for instance, Contract Law, Employment Law, Company Law, or Consumer Law without a reasonable appreciation of the effects of European Law.

The topics covered in *Key Facts: EU Law* include all of the main areas of all mainstream syllabuses. When it is studied in the context of the substantive law, EU Law is actually a very exiting and developing area of law.

A Table identifying the different numbering of Treaty Articles prior to the Treaty of Amsterdam and after the Treaty of Lisbon is included at the end of the book.

The law is as I believe it to be on 1st October 2010.

KEY FACTS

EU LAW

3rd edition

Chris Turner

Bromley Libraries

ER
ON

TE UK COMPANY

Orders: please contact Bookpoint Ltd, 130 Milton Park, Abingdon, Oxon OX14 4SB.
Telephone: (44) 01235 827720. Fax: (44) 01235 400454. Lines are open from 9.00–5.00, Monday
to Saturday, with a 24-hour message answering service. You can also order through
our website www.hoddereducation.co.uk

British Library Cataloguing in Publication Data
A catalogue record for this title is available from The British Library.

ISBN 978 1 444 11089 0

First published 2002
Second Edition 2006
Third Edition 2011
Impression number   10 9 8 7 6 5 4 3 2 1
Year   2014 2013 2012 2011

Copyright © 2002, 2006, 2011 Chris Turner
All rights reserved. No part of this publication may be reproduced or transmitted in any
form or by any means, electronic or mechanical, including photocopy, recording, or any
information storage and retrieval system, without permission in writing from the publisher or
under licence from the Copyright Licensing Agency Limited. Further details of such licences
(for reprographic reproduction) may be obtained from the Copyright Licensing Agency
Limited, Saffron House, 6–10 Kirby Street, London, EC1N 8TS.

Hachette UK's policy is to use papers that are natural, renewable and recyclable products and
made from wood grown in sustainable forests. The logging and manufacturing processes are
expected to conform to the environmental regulations of the country of origin.

Typeset by Transet Limited, Coventry, Warwickshire.
Printed in Great Britain for Hodder Education, an Hachette UK Company, 338 Euston Road,
London NW1 3BH by Cox & Wyman Ltd, Reading, Berks.

1

The constitution and character of EU law

1.1 Origins and background

1.1.1 The concept of a single Europe

1. The UK tends towards 'euro-scepticism', so two misconceptions usually prevail:
   - that the idea of a united Europe is new;
   - that the EU legal order is a haphazard process of co-operation between Member States.

2. The Roman Empire is one possible starting point, with several subsequent attempts at European unity or aspirations towards it:
   - Papal view of 'Christendom';
   - Charlemagne's 'Holy Roman Empire';
   - Henry IV of France and the 'Christian Commonwealth of Europe';
   - and even the aspirations of Napoleon and Hitler;
   - European unity has also been a common theme of every major political philosopher, e.g. Kant, Rousseau, Neitzsche, Marx.

3. So history possibly favours the 'europhiles', with 'euro-scepticism' a more recent nationalist hostility to the EU.

4. Ironically, a federal Europe originated as a British idea.

5. The intellectual architect of 'Europe' was Jean Monnet.

1.1.2 The background to the European Union (Community)

1. There were various attempts at integration in the 19th and 20th centuries.

2. These were based on need to avoid war, particularly after the Second World War.

3. There were two key factors:
   - the Treaty of Versailles failed and led to rise of Nazism;

■ so it was vital to bring Germany within the European 'partnership'.

4. Churchill, in his 1947 Zurich speech, said 'We must build a kind of United States of Europe'.

5. The European Union of Federalists was established in 1947.

6. Continental advocates of union argued for 'supranational bodies' in the Montreux Resolution 1947.

7. Various intergovernmental agreements created new world or European organisations at this time: IMF; GATT; OEEC; The Council of Europe; Benelux Union.

1.1.3 The creation of the Treaties

1. The Treaties originated in the 'Schumann Plan' following principles established in the 'Marshall Plan' in the USA:
   ■ the narrow aspect was placing French and German coal and steel production under a 'higher authority';
   ■ the wider agenda was to move towards a federal Europe.

2. The plan led to the first Treaty: European Coal and Steel Community Treaty (ECSC Treaty) – Treaty of Paris 1951.
   ■ It also devised an institutional framework of communities (later to be added to by European Court of Justice).
   ■ Monnet was made first President of ECSC.

3. This was followed by an unsuccessful initiative to create a European Defence Community.

4. Further integration and a move towards the establishment of supranational institutions came with the two Treaties of Rome 1957 – the European Atomic Energy Community Treaty (EURATOM), and the European Economic Community Treaty (EC Treaty).

5. The latter resulted from the Spaak Committee Report and a recommendation for the creation of a 'common market'.

6. The Treaties were originally signed by only six countries: France, Italy, Germany, Belgium, The Netherlands and Luxembourg.
   ■ Different countries had different things to gain.
   ■ This meant that integration was always dogged by national self-interest.
   ■ This ensured that development would be 'incremental' and that principle would be sacrificed to pragmatism.
   ■ As a result, the UK stayed out.

7. Objectives of the Treaties were to be achieved by two means:
   - the creation of a common market and common policies;
   - monetary union.

8. The former has always predominated and dictated the character of the Community.

9. So, the establishment of the 'four freedoms', the removal of internal barriers and, more importantly, the new legal order were required.

1.2 The development of the Treaties (from EC, ECSC, EURATOM, to SEA, TEU, ToA, ToN and ToL)

1. The original Treaties have been supplemented and modified, firstly within the Community and then in an evolving Union.

2. The early years of the Community, from 1958 to 1965, were characterised by economic boom:
   - good progress was made towards the creation of a 'customs union', i.e. dismantling of tariffs;
   - but there was far less progress towards an actual common market;
   - some competition policy was put in place;
   - some moves were made towards free movement of workers;
   - but there was over-prominence of the Common Agricultural Policy (CAP);
   - good work was done by the European Court of Justice (ECJ) in defining the character of the legal order.

3. The Common Market should have been achieved within the 'transitional period', i.e.12 years from 1957, in three four-year periods.

4. However, in 1965–66 DeGaulle created a crisis over qualified majority voting, with France withdrawing from participation in the Council.

5. This was partly resolved by the Luxembourg Accords, which effectively created a sort of veto for Member States on major issues (of uncertain future with commitment to integration in the Treaty on European Union).

6. In many ways the years from then until 1986 and the adoption of the Single European Act (SEA) are seen as years of stagnation in terms of integration.

- This can partly be explained by economic recession and the retreat into national interest (particularly the UK).
- However, in other areas the community did develop:
 (i) by enlargement (firstly to 12, then to 15 countries);
 (ii) by broadening (developing policy in and outside the original Treaty objectives – although some took some time to be fully adopted because of national self-interest, e.g. Social Charter);
 (iii) judicial activism of the ECJ (in defining supremacy and developing direct effect and its alternatives).

7. The effective 're-launch' of the Community came in 1986.

8. There were three principal reasons for this:
 - the Commission presidency of Jacques Delors;
 - a commitment to further integration by key political figures in the Member States (notably Chancellor Kohl in Germany and President Mitterand in France);
 - the growing realisation that survival depended on an effective EC;
 - the adoption of the Single European Act (with a set time scale of 1992 for implementation of the Single Market).

9. SEA 1986 included five major provisions:
 - a definition of the internal market and the 1992 deadline;
 - a new law-making process in co-operation with Parliament on certain measures;
 - creation of the Court of First Instance to support the ECJ;
 - provision for compulsory rather than *ad hoc* meetings of a European Council twice yearly (formally recognised);
 - the idea of European Political Co-operation.

10. Treaty on European Union (TEU) (signed at Maastricht) followed in 1992.
 - It did not include everything most states wanted.
 - The UK was allowed to opt out of the most important parts in order to secure a treaty at all.
 - So the desired environmental laws were not included.
 - There was only agreement to co-operate on defence and justice, rather than being part of the legal order.
 - Eleven of the then 12 agreed on the Social Chapter, but the UK opted out, thus necessitating the protocol procedure.
 - But it did create the union and the idea of European citizenship – though not within the legal order.

11. The Treaty of Amsterdam 1997 then re-numbered the Articles of the EC Treaty, and the UK signed the Social Chapter.

12. The Treaty of Nice introduced major changes to the composition of the institutions, voting procedures, enlargement and 'enhanced co-operation'.

13. A draft constitution to put all aspects of the EU within the legal order was accepted as the EU Constitution. Some states ratified it by parliamentary vote but it was rejected in referenda in France and the Netherlands, leaving some doubt as to how the EU would develop. A 'two-track Europe' is one possibility.

14. The Lisbon Treaty introduced similar modifications to the Treaties, but without the single constitutional document. The Treaty is now in force.

1.3 Basic aims and objectives of EU law and supranationalism

1. The objectives of the EU are quite simply stated in the EC Treaty (now TFEU), as amended and built on by later Treaties: 'to promote throughout the community (now EU) a harmonious development of economic activities, a continuous, balanced expansion, an increase in stability, an accelerated raising of the standard of living and quality of life and closer relations between the states belonging to it and sustainable development of economic activities, a high level of employment and of social protection, equality between men and women, sustainable and non-inflationary growth, a high degree of competitiveness and convergence of economic performance, a high level of protection and of improvement of the quality of the environment, and economic and social cohesion among the Member States.'

2. It is easy to assume that the constitution of the EU is no more than what is laid down in the Treaties, but this would be only partly true because all constitutions are defined by how they are interpreted in the Courts.

3. The EU constitution has the added complication of being founded in Treaty relationships entered into by sovereign states (one reason why the EU tried to create a written EU Constitution).

4. So, the first problem is identifying how Treaties come to be incorporated in Member States' law. There are two approaches:
   - Monist constitutions – these include France and the Netherlands. The Treaty is automatically incorporated into the national legal system at the point of ratification.
   - Dualist constitutions – these include Germany, Italy, Belgium and, of course, the UK where the Treaty is only incorporated after enactment. (In the UK this was by the European Communities Act 1972.)

5. The result can be a wide variance in how the Treaties are interpreted and applied.

6. For the legal order of the EU to function, the institutions must be 'supranational', i.e. in relation to those things covered by the Treaties, they take precedence over national institutions.

7. The ECJ, in administering and defining EU law, and the principle of 'supranationalism' become vital to the role of ensuring the universal application of the Treaties:
   - 'To avoid disparities arising out of different national approaches to the incorporation of EC (now EU) law and to ensure uniformity in its application, the Court of Justice has developed its own jurisprudence on the Supremacy of EC (now EU) law.' (Penelope Kent: *The Law of the European Union*, Longman)
   - 'ECJ has uniformly and consistently been the most effective integration institution in the EU. Its role was established in Art 164 (now repealed): "The Court shall ensure that in the interpretation and application of this Treaty the law is observed." From its very inception in the Treaty, the ECJ set about establishing its hierarchical authority as the ultimate court of constitutional review. In this area two areas in particular are important. First there is the role of the ECJ in controlling member state courts, and, second, there is the role of the Court in managing the incessant inter-institutional struggles.' (Ian Ward: *A Critical Introduction to European Law*, Butterworths)

8. In respect of the former of these two – defining the relationship between the Community legal order and the Member States – three crucial factors apply:
   - the doctrine of Supremacy (or Primacy) of EU law;
   - the Art 267 reference procedure;
   - the doctrine of direct effect.

9. More recently, indirect effect and state liability have also been developed by the ECJ to ensure that citizens can enforce their rights.

1.4 The European Union

1.4.1 General

1. The European Union finally came into force in 1993, only after ratification of the TEU by Member States.

2. The TEU created an entirely new structure, over and above that of the EC.

3. Between ToN and ToL, the constitution was described as the 'three pillars':
   - Pillar 1: comprised the legal order of the original Treaties, added to by economic and monetary union – so the other pillars are outside the scope of the legal order.
   - Pillar 2: co-operation towards common foreign and security policy.
   - Pillar 3: Police and judicial co-operation in criminal matters (originally co-operation towards common systems on justice and home affairs).

4. Pillars 2 and 3 are found in Titles V and VI and were not specifically incorporated into UK law.

5. There was debate over whether it was accurate to speak of EU law rather than EC law. Since the two extra pillars created by TEU had no foundation in law but were based on co-operation, and since the law stemmed from the EC Treaty not the TEU, it was probably most accurate to use EC to refer to law, and EU to refer to the geographical unit formed by the 27 states.

6. Following the Treaty of Lisbon, all three pillars are incorporated into the Union with the same force and there is now e.g. a High Representative of the Union for Foreign Affairs and Security Policy.

1.4.2 The institutions of the Union

1. Before the Treaty of Lisbon there were strictly speaking no EU institutions, these were EC institutions. Now they are all institutions of the EU.

2. Article 3 (now repealed) of TEU provides that 'The Union shall be served by a single institutional framework …'.

3. Following the Treaty of Lisbon, the institutions are now the institutions of the EU with mostly the powers and duties proscribed for them under the original EC treaty.

1.4.3 The objectives of the Union

1. The objectives of the original Treaties were modified and amended over time by SEA and then TEU.

2. The objectives of the EU after ToL are:
   - free movement of citizens;
   - establishment of the internal market;
   - balanced economic growth;
   - a competitive social market economy;
   - full employment, social progress;
   - protection of the environment;
   - promotion of scientific and technological advance;
   - combating social exclusion and discrimination;
   - promotion of social justice;
   - equality between men and women;
   - protection of the rights of children;
   - promotion of economic, social and territorial cohesion;
   - respect for cultural and linguistic diversity;
   - economic and monetary union.

1.4.4 Common foreign and security policies

1. Between the TEU and ToL, this was Pillar 2 of the EU based on co-operation between Member States rather than having the legal force of the Community.

2. Now the ToL has merged the three pillars although special procedures exist.

3. There is also now a High Representative of the Union for Foreign Affairs and Security Policy – the role of which includes:
   - conducting common foreign and security policy (Art 18(2) TEU);
   - chairing the Foreign Affairs Council (Art 18(3) TEU);
   - acting as a Vice-President of the Commission (Art 18(4) TEU).

4. By Art 24(2) TEU the EU is to pursue common policies and work for a high degree of co-operation in international relations – and by Art 26(1) TEU the European Council sets out the strategic interests.

5. Common foreign and security policy now includes:
   - a solidarity clause in the event of terrorism;
   - that international agreements can be made with one or more states or international organisations.
6. Art 42 TEU provides for a common security and defence policy including sharing military assets.

1.4.5 Area of freedom, security and justice

1. This was first introduced in TEU as the third pillar as 'Justice and Home Affairs' and was later changed in ToA to 'Police and judicial co-operation in criminal matters.
2. Now it is referred to in Art 20 TEU and in Arts 67–89 TFEU.
3. It includes such areas as immigration and asylum seeking – Art 80 TFEU, and judicial co-operation in criminal matters – Art 83(1) TFEU.
4. Art 67(1) TFEU recognises respect for the 'fundamental rights and different legal systems and traditions of Member States.'
5. Legislation is now by the Ordinary Legislative Procedure (formerly the co-decision procedure) and is by qualified majority voting.

1.4.6 Final provisions of the TEU

1. The EC Treaty provided simple mechanisms for amending certain issues.
2. Now, other amendments must be made through TEU procedure:
   - the Commission or Member State submits an amendment to the Council;
   - the Council decides to hold an intergovernmental conference after consulting with the Commission and Parliament;
   - a unanimous vote in the conference results in the amendment being sent to Member States for ratification.
3. Accession is to the Union:
   - there are a number of other potential applicants: Albania, Bosnia and Herzegovina, Kosovo, Montenegro and Serbia;
   - applications require unanimous approval of Council and assent of Parliament;
   - current applications for membership include Turkey and Croatia;

- the Commission has stated that applicants fulfilling the necessary criteria should be eligible for entry after 2002 – Turkey's application has been unsuccessful so far because of its human rights record.

4. As in the EC Treaty, there is no mention of secession, and there are no mechanisms for withdrawal, which contradicts the UK's position on parliamentary supremacy.

1.4.7 Some criticisms of the TEU

1. The UK reduced the scope of the Treaty by opting out of almost all the positive parts.

2. This led to fragmentation and the creation of various protocols, described by some commentators as having no basis in the legal order.

3. So, Maastricht was a surrender to national interests, e.g. subsidiarity, but this seems contradictory as Union is a concept that implies a federal system.

4. The 'democratic deficit' was increased, not decreased:
   - the Commission was still powerful, and still undemocratic;
   - Parliament was increasingly democratic, but still relatively ineffective;
   - the Council was still the major power;
   - so supranationalism was once again sacrificed for national interests.

2

The institutions of the European Union

The Council

- Fluid membership depending on subject discussed.
- The real law maker.
- Law is passed by qualified majority voting or unanimous voting, e.g. in developing Treaties.

Commission

- 'Civil service' with 24,000 staff.
- 27 Commissioners at present, each with Directorates General.
- Has three principal roles: drafting legislaion; 'watchdog' of the Treaties; executive functions, e.g. implementing policy.

Parliament

- Democratically elected – numbers of MEPs based on importance of state.
- Consultative and amending role in legislation.
- Can censure Commission and affect non-compulsory budget.

THE INSTITUTIONS

Other institutions

- The General Court – helps ECJ, e.g. staff cases.
- COREPER helps prepare Ministers for Council work.
- Committee of Regions and Economic and Social Committee – consultation.
- Court of Auditors – reviews expenditure.
- European Council – twice-yearly summit.

European Court of Justice

27 *Judges Rapporteurs* plus Advocates-General:
- hear Art 267 referrals from Member States; and
- Art 258 infringement actions against Member States; and
- Art 263 (abuse of powers), Art 265 (failure to act), Art 340 (action for damages) against institutions.

2.1 The development of the Institutions

1. Concept and character of the institutions begins with the ECSC.

2. This required supranational bodies working independently of the Member States.

3. The ECSC introduced the idea of 'community', with the following main features:
   - distinct legal personality;
   - represented by autonomous institutions;
   - Member States ceded some national sovereignty to institutions for defined purposes.

4. The first institution was the 'High Authority', with power to make legally binding decisions.
   - Supplemented by a 'Common Assembly' – representative of Member States.
   - Added to by a 'Special Council of Ministers' – with some legislative powers.
   - Completed initially by a 'Court of Justice' to 'ensure that the law was observed'.

5. EEC and EURATOM Treaties followed the same pattern.
   - Establishing 'communities' with four key institutions.
   - High Authority was replaced by a Commission with more limited powers.

6. A convention at the same time created a single Assembly and a single Court of Justice to represent all three communities.

7. The Brussels Treaty 1967 (Merger Treaty) established a single Council, and High Authority and two Commissions merged into one Commission – but communities kept separate identities.

8. The EU has a unique institutional structure:
   - it is not like any international organisation;
   - nor like a parliamentary democracy;
   - it has no clear separation of powers, but does have separation of interests;
   - it has a complex legislative process and an executive without real executive powers;
   - its institutions all have broad autonomy and their own rules of procedure;

- but the overriding ruler of the community is the Treaties – everything must conform with their objectives;
- and the Court of Justice exercises supervisory jurisdiction.

9. The Institutions have been added to over the years:
   - Art 4 EC Treaty led to an Economic and Social Committee and a Court of Auditors – made independent by TEU;
   - Art 4 also allowed COREPER – Committee of Permanent Representatives;
   - SEA established the Court of First Instance;
   - TEU created a Committee of the Regions;
   - TEU also provided for a European Investment Bank and European Central Bank.

10. The role of the Institutions has also gradually changed:
    - new Institutions have added complexity but not necessarily improvement;
    - the balance of power between Council and Commission has shifted;
    - Council's powers have increased;
    - Parliament's role has increased.

2.2 The Council

1. This was formerly referred to as the Council of Ministers – after TEU it was the Council of the European Union; after ToL it is now the Council.

2. The Council is a fluid concept with floating membership:
   - 'Council consists of authorised representatives of each state';
   - the identity of the Minister depends on the subject of discussion;
   - but the original intention was a college of delegates.

3. ToL creates the concept of Team Presidencies for different configurations of Council other than foreign affairs.

4. The Council is the major legislative organ, although there are some exceptions. It consults Parliament and Economic and Social Committees, but makes the final decision on any legislation.

5. The voting procedure is of two main types:
   - unanimous – required for certain prescribed areas and, since Luxembourg Accords, if vital national interests at stake;
   - qualified majority – with minimum of 255 votes (representing 62% of the EU population) carrying a measure, so designed to prevent large states abusing small ones, but originally designed to be used *per se*.

6. The qualified majority system is based on differential weighting according to the size and influence of the state:

Germany, France, Italy, UK	29 votes each
Spain, Poland	27 votes each
Romania	14 votes
Netherlands	13 votes
Belgium, Czech Republic, Greece, Hungary, Portugal	12 votes each
Austria, Bulgaria, Sweden	10 votes each
Denmark, Ireland, Lithunaia, Slovakia, Finland	7 votes each
Cyprus, Estonia, Latvia, Luxembourg, Slovenia	4 votes each
Malta	3 votes

7. The Council has as its objective, 'to ensure that the objectives set out in the Treaty are attained'.

8. But of course it is also a political body actually representing the interests of the individual Member States.

9. The Council is supplemented by two further processes:
   - European Council: twice-yearly meetings of heads of state and Foreign Ministers – a political summit;
   - COREPER: a permanent committee representing Member States – sifting through Commission proposals.

2.3 The European Commission

1. The Commission has the clearest claim to being a supranational body.

2. It is sometimes referred to as a civil service, but has much broader powers and roles.

3. It is currently composed of 27 Commissioners:
   - by Art 245 one from each state;

- chosen on grounds of general competence and 'whose independence is beyond doubt';
- they take an oath to be independent and not seek or take instructions from their Member State (Art 245);
- their Member State undertakes not to influence them;
- the appointment is for a five-year term;
- each Commissioner gets a Directorate General with specific responsibilities;
- the Commission also includes 24,000 staff.

4. The Commission is headed by a President, who holds office for a renewable two-year period.

5. The Commission is collegiate and acts by simple majority.

6. It has three principal responsibilities:
   - it is initiator of legislation under Art 352 and can draft proposals on anything covered by the Treaties;
   - it is watchdog of the Treaties – all Member States are obliged to achieve the objectives of the Treaties, and the Commission can deal with breaches of EU law by Member States through Art 258 proceedings;
   - it has executive functions, for instance the Commission is responsible for implementing policy and also for the compulsory budget.

7. Through a process known as comity the Council can delegate power to the Commission, i.e. to produce detailed regulations following the passing of a framework regulation by the Council.

8. The Commission is sometimes also accountable to Parliament, e.g. Parliament can pass a motion of censure causing the Commission to resign.

2.4 The European Parliament

1. This was originally known as the Assembly.
   - It was not democratically elected.
   - It comprised appointed nominees from Member State governments.
   - It had no legislative power and was only consultative.

2. It has been an elected body since 1979.
   - Elections are every five years.
   - Total membership is 736.

3. Membership depends on the size and importance of the particular Member State:

Member State	Number of MEPs each
Germany	99
France, Italy, UK	72
Poland, Spain	50
Romania	33
Netherlands	25
Belgium, Greece, Portugal, Czech Republic, Hungary	22
Sweden	18
Austria	17
Bulgaria	17
Denmark, Finland, Slovakia	13
Ireland, Lithuania	12
Latvia	8
Slovenia	7
Cyprus, Estonia, Luxembourg	6
Malta	5

4. These MEPs were elected before ToL which will increase the number to 754.

5. MEPs sit by political groupings rather than by national interest, and there is no mandatory voting for Member State interests – MEPs are representatives, not delegates.

6. Voting is on a majority basis.

7. Parliament elects its own President and officials

8. Parliament enjoys three main powers at present:
   - it can censure the Commission (and such a censure in 1999 led to the resignation of the entire Commission);

- it has powers over the non-compulsory budget;
- it has a consultative role in legislation mostly through the co-decision procedure.

2.5 The Court of Justice

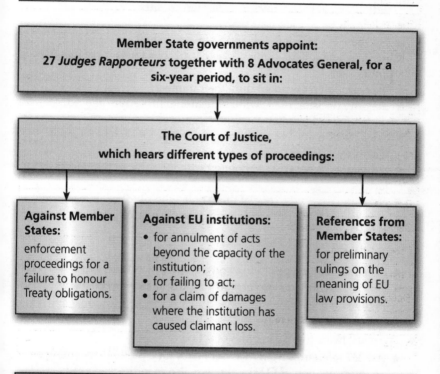

Member State governments appoint:
27 *Judges Rapporteurs* together with 8 Advocates General, for a six-year period, to sit in:

The Court of Justice,
which hears different types of proceedings:

Against Member States:
enforcement proceedings for a failure to honour Treaty obligations.

Against EU institutions:
- for annulment of acts beyond the capacity of the institution;
- for failing to act;
- for a claim of damages where the institution has caused claimant loss.

References from Member States:
for preliminary rulings on the meaning of EU law provisions.

The General Court (12 judges) hears different actions:
- direct actions by natural and legal persons (not anti-dumping);
- staff cases;
- some references for preliminary rulings.

The work of the ECJ and General Court

1. This is not like any court in the English legal system.

2. It is composed of 27 *Judges Rapporteurs* (the judges) and these are assisted by eight Advocates General:
   - one judge is appointed from each state;
   - by Art 253 TFEU they must be independent beyond doubt and judges or legal academics in their own country;
   - they each serve a six-year term;
   - but there is a staggered re-appointment system;
   - removal of a judge is only possible if all colleagues agree that (s)he is unfit to serve;
   - they appoint a president from their number;
   - majority decision rules, with inquisitorial procedure and no dissenting judgments;
   - cases used to involve a full count but often ToN can be a Grand Chamber of fewer judges;
   - Advocates General are appointed with the same requirements as for judges;
   - cases are assigned to one of these first, who produces a reasoned opinion for the court – this does not have to be followed by the court but it may be.

3. The role of the court is:
   - to ensure that in application and interpretation the law is observed;
   - and to provide a forum for resolving disputes between institutions, Member States, and individuals;
   - and to protect individual rights.

4. The court hears five main types of action:
   - Art 267 references from Member States for a preliminary ruling on an interpretation of EU law (known also as indirect actions);
   - Art 258 actions against Member States for failing to implement Treaty obligations (a direct action known also as infringement proceedings);
   - Art 263 actions against an institution for abuse of power;
   - Art 265 actions against an institution for a failure to act;
   - Art 340 actions for damages against an institution that has been responsible for loss to the individual, e.g. where the Commission has failed to address a decision to a body engaging in anti-competitive practices and an individual suffers loss as a result.

5. It is important to note that the ECJ has been responsible for defining the Treaties and in particular has been instrumental in ensuring their

enforcement through many landmark decisions, e.g. defining and developing the principles of supremacy, direct effect, indirect effect, state liability, etc.

6. Because of the excess workload of the ECJ and resultant delays, SEA also created a Court of First Instance (now the General Court):
   - it has similar requirements to the ECJ;
   - its basic purpose is to ease the workload of the ECJ (but has had limited success in doing so);
   - it only takes on limited specific cases, e.g. staff cases;
   - Art 267 references on limited range of specific areas;
   - there is a possible right of appeal to the ECJ.

2.6 The other major institutions

1. Besides the four main Institutions of Council, Commission, Parliament and European Court of Justice, there are a number of other important Institutions – the first three have already been referred to

2. The European Council:
   - a twice-yearly summit of the heads of state and Foreign Ministers, focusing on political matters;
   - in 1999 it gave a brief to the intergovernmental conference (IGC) to keep under review: the size and composition of the EU; weighting of votes in the Council of Ministers; extension to qualified majority voting.

3. COREPER – the Committee of Permanent Representatives:
   - It is a permanent body of representatives from Member States, because of the fluid membership of the Council.
   - It examines the Commission's legislative proposals for individual Ministers.

4. The General Court:
   - set up initially in SEA;
   - usually sits with three or five judges;
   - jurisdiction was limited to staff cases, competition cases and anti-dumping cases but has been extended;
   - since 1993 it can hear all cases brought by natural or legal persons (including judicial review), but not those brought by the institutions or by the Member States.

5. The Court of Auditors:
   - This was created in 1975.
   - It was designed to control and supervise the community budget.
   - It was made a full institution by TEU.
   - It has qualified members from each state.
   - It examines accounts of all revenue and expenditure.

6. The Economic and Social Committee (ESC):
   - Membership is based on representation of social and economic activities, e.g. farmers, carriers, dealers, craftsmen, etc.
   - It has a consultative role within the EU.
   - It is consulted by either the Council or the Commission wherever they deem that it is appropriate to consult.
   - It has a maximum of 350 members who are appointed by the Council.

7. The Committee of the Regions:
   - This came into being in 1994 after TEU.
   - It has membership comes from local and regional bodies, but not local or national government.
   - It has a maximum of 350 members.
   - It has a consultative role and is designed to bring regional influence to EU legislation.
   - It usually gives opinions on things like education and training, culture, health, environmental issues and social cohesion.

8. The European Central Bank (ECB):
   - In TEU provision was made in the Protocol to have a Central Bank to act for the EU.
   - It is obviously a vital element of economic monetary union and the single currency.
   - From January 1999 it has had responsibility for monetary policy in the EU.
   - It is the only body allowed to issue euro banknotes.

3

The sources of European law

Primary Sources	The Treaties:	
	ECSC; EURATOM; EC; SEA; TEU; ToA; ToN; ToL. Divides into: • Procedural Treaty Articles, e.g. Art 288 which identifies the legislation; or Art 258 an action against a Member State. • Substantive Treaty Articles, e.g. Art 157 Equal pay for men and women; or Art 45 the free movement of workers.	
Secondary Sources	**Legislation:**	
	Regulations	Automatically law in Member States. They are generally applicable, binding in their entirety, and directly applicable.
	Directives	Binding as to the effect to be achieved. Member States have an implementing period within which they must be incorporated in national law by whatever method.
	Decisions	Addressed to a specific party, whether a company, individual, or Member State. They are then binding in their entirety on the party to whom they are addressed.
	Recommendations	Have no legal force but are persuasive.
	Opinions	Have no legal force but are persuasive.
Tertiary Sources	**Case law of European Court of Justice**	
	Vital because of: • the power to ensure observance of Treaty objectives through Art 267 references; • the judicial creativity of the ECJ in comparison to the relative inertia of the legislative bodies.	
	General Principles:	
	• proportionality, equality, legal certainty; • protection of fundamental human rights; • subsidiarity.	
	Acts adopted by representatives of Member State Governments meeting in Council.	
	National law of Member States.	
	Public International law.	

The sources of EU law

3.1 Primary sources – the Treaties

3.1.1 The structure of the Treaty on the Functioning of the European Union (replacing EC Treaty)

1. This begins with a preamble, which is useful for the ECJ for interpretation purposes.

2. It is then split into seven parts:
   - principles – ground rules;
   - citizenship – added by TEU and now in Art 20;
   - policies of the Community – effectively the legal order;
   - references to overseas relationships;
   - external action by the Union;
   - the institutions – empowerment and identification of roles, etc.;
   - general and final provisions, e.g. to enter into other treaties.

3. It also includes annexes, protocols and declarations.

4. The substantive law of the Treaty is also contained in numerous Articles.

3.1.2 The principles

1. Following ToL Art 3 TEU has replaced Arts 2 and 3 EC Treaty and covers the basic principles and objectives of the EU.

2. The principles include:
   - promoting peace and the well-being of the people;
   - offering citizens an area of freedom, security and juistice without internal frontiers;
   - free movement of citizens recognising external border controls, immigration and asylum, and prevention of crime.

3. Objectives include:
   - establishment of the internal market;
   - balanced economic growth;
   - a competitive social market economy;
   - full employment, social progress;
   - protection of the environment;
   - promotion of scientific and technological advance;
   - combating social exclusion and discrimination;
   - promotion of social justice;

- equality between men and women;
- protection of the rights of children;
- promotion of economic, social and territorial cohesion;
- respect for cultural and linguistic diversity;
- economic and monetary union.

4. Art 3 TEU seeks to ensure that the EU acts within the limits of its powers and for the objectives assigned to it.

5. Art 4(3) TEU identifies the obligations of the Member States:
   - 'to take all appropriate measures ... to ensure fulfillment of the objectives arising out of the Treaty ...';
   - 'to abstain from any measure which could jeopardise the attainment of the objectives ...'.

6. Art 18 TFEU identifies basic principle of non-discrimination on the basis of nationality.

3.1.3 The Union policies

1. These are found in Part 3.

2. The most important are the 'Four Freedoms':
   - free movement of goods (agriculture as a special category);
   - free movement of persons;
   - free movement of services (transport as a special category);
   - free movement of capital.

3. Free movement of goods provides for the elimination of customs duties and quantitative restrictions between Member States to products originating in Member States, and products coming from non-Member States that are 'in free circulation':
   - Art 30 governs the Customs Union – elimination of duties, etc.;
   - Art 34 and Art 35 cover non-tariff barriers – elimination of quotas and bans.

4. Agriculture is subject to complex rules and a Common Agricultural Policy (CAP).

5. Free movement of persons and services are both guaranteed under the Treaties in Art 45, Art 49 and Art 56, and workers' families are also given protections in secondary legislation.

6. A common transport policy is also envisaged in the Treaty.

7. Free movement of capital is contained in TEU, all restrictions on movement of capital and payments is prohibited, and now policy is ultimately driven towards economic and monetary union.

8. Other main EU policies include:
   - rules on anti-competitive practices in Art 101 and Art 102;
   - tax provisions in Art 110;
   - anti-discrimination in A157.

3.1.4 Rules on the institutions and on procedure

1. One of the most important procedural Articles is Art 288, which identifies and explains the different forms of legislation.

2. The relationship with Member States is partly defined in Art 267, which provides the mechanism for gaining interpretations of EU law from the ECJ.

3. The general rules regarding each of the institutions are in the TFEU:
   - Parliament in Arts 223–234;
   - Council in Arts 237–243;
   - Commission in Arts 244–250;
   - Court of Justice in Arts 251–281.

3.1.5 The general and final provisions

1. Provides EU with a legal personality – so under Art 354 it can make arrangements with other international bodies.

2. The EU can be liable through its institutions (Art 340).

3. Powers are also given to Member States to derogate from Treaty obligations in certain extreme circumstances, e.g. security, serious internal disturbance or threat of external conflict, balance of payments crises.

4. The Council has very broad powers under Art 352 to legislate to do anything that is 'necessary to attain ... an objective of the EU ...'.

3.2 Secondary sources – Regulations, Directives and Decisions

3.2.1 The acts of the Institutions

1. Secondary legislation is a collective term used to describe all the various types of law the Institutions can make.

2. They are subordinate to primary law (the Treaties), and so cannot amend, repeal or alter the scope of a primary instrument.

3. So the Institutions may only act:
   - in order to carry out their tasks;
   - in strict accordance with the provisions of the Treaties;
   - within the limits of the powers conferred upon them in the Treaties, specifically Art 288.

4. The TFEU at Art 288 provides that: 'In order to carry out their tasks and in accordance with the provisions of this Treaty, the European Parliament acting jointly with the Council [added by TEU], the Council and the Commission shall make regulations and issue directives, take decisions, make recommendations or deliver opinions.'

5. The various forms of secondary legislation are described in Art 288 and it is their scope and effect that distinguishes them from each other.

3.2.2 Regulations

1. By Art 288: 'A regulation shall have general application. It shall be binding in its entirety and directly applicable in all Member States.'
   - 'General application' means it applies to all Member States.
   - 'Binding in its entirety' means Member States have no choice but to give effect to the regulation in its entirety.
   - 'Directly applicable' means the regulation automatically becomes law in each Member State with no requirement for the state to do anything to implement it, and it may create rights and obligations directly enforceable in the national courts (*Bussone v Ministry of Agriculture* (1978)).

2. Regulations enter into force on the date specified in them.

3.2.3 Directives

1. By Art 288: 'A directive shall be binding, as to the result to be achieved, upon each Member State to which it is addressed, but shall leave to the national authorities the choice of form and methods.'

2. Directives are unlike regulations (which are uniform and directly applicable rules):
   - they are used to ensure that Member States adapt their own laws for the application of common standards;
   - they require Member States to choose the method of implementation within a set deadline;
   - they are mainly used in areas where the diversity of national laws could have a harmful effect on the establishment or functioning of the Single Market.

3. So, whereas a regulation is applicable to Member States and individual citizens alike, a directive:
   - is primarily intended to create legal obligations on the Member State;
   - so is not intended to create directly enforceable rights for individuals, but the ECJ ensures that it does.

4. However, there are now important exceptions to this last point:
   - vertical direct effect, which may be relied upon by the individual in the case of unimplemented directives if the claim is against the state or an 'emanation of the state' (*van Duyn* and *Ratti* and, of course, *Marshall* and, for an indication of what amounts to an emanation of the state, see also UK cases such as *Foster v British Gas* and *Doughty v Rolls-Royce*);
   - the duty of 'uniform interpretation', which the ECJ derives originally from Art 10 EC Treaty. Where there is a divergence between national law and the directive, the national law must be interpreted so as to give effect to the directive even where it remains unimplemented (the *Von Colson* principle, as developed by *Marleasing*) – the so-called principle of 'indirect effect');
   - the *Francovich* principle, that while there can be no horizontal direct effect based on a directive as between non-state parties, an individual who has suffered loss as a result of the Member State's failure to implement a directive may claim damages from the state (so-called 'state liability' – *Grad v Finanzamt Traustein 9/70*).

3.2.4 Decisions

1. By Art 288: 'A decision shall be binding in its entirety upon those to whom it is addressed.'

2. The first feature of a decision is that it is the least easy to define of the legislative acts – it could be a legally binding measure in a specific legal form, but it could also be a non-binding, informal act laying down guidelines.

3. Its most striking effect is that it is immediately and totally binding on the addressee, and as a result may create rights for third parties.

	General applicability	Direct applicability	Direct effect
Treaty articles	Yes – they apply throughout the community	Once Treaty is incorporated there is no need for further enactment of Articles	Yes – if they conform to the *Van Gend* criteria
Regulations	Yes – they apply throughout the community	Yes – they require no further implementation	Yes – if they conform to the *Van Gend* criteria
Directives	Yes – they will be addressed to all states	No – they are an order, so require implementation	Only vertically if unimplemented or incorrectly implemented
Decisions	No – they are addressed to a particular individual	They are an order that must be complied with by the addressee	They may confer rights on other individuals affected by them

The effects of primary and secondary law

3.3 The process of legislating

3.3.1 Introduction

1. The process of legislating has been modified significantly as the result of different Treaties – one of the most significant features of the early legislative process was the so-called 'democratic deficit'.

2. Prior to the Treaty of Lisbon, there were four types of legislative procedure:
   - the proposal (or consultation) procedure;
   - the co-operation procedure;
   - the co-decision procedure;
   - assent.

3. The proposal procedure was the original legislative procedure in existence before the SEA.

4. Following SEA the co-operation procedure was introduced to provide a straightforward method, involving the European Parliament (two readings) and to be passed by qualified majority voting for internal market measures – in fact this was largely removed by the Treaty of Amsterdam, and only survived in respect of EMU.

5. TEU introduced the co-decision procedure, which was subsequently modified or simplified by ToA and, as the Ordinary Legislative Procedure, is now the main method of legislating following ToL.

6. The assent procedure, which was similar to the co-decision procedure, was introduced first in SEA and extended by TEU.

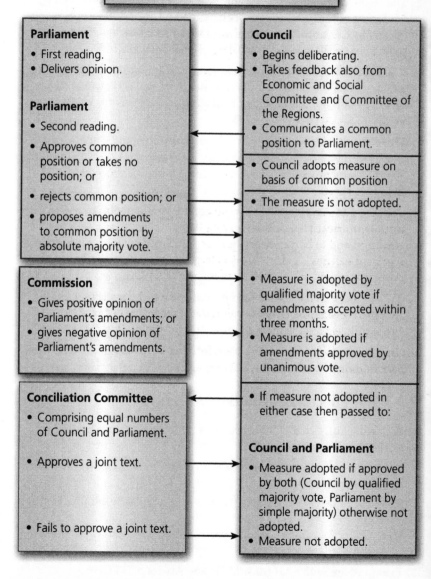

Commission

Produces draft proposal and sends it to:

Parliament
- First reading.
- Delivers opinion.

Parliament
- Second reading.
- Approves common position or takes no position; or
- rejects common position; or
- proposes amendments to common position by absolute majority vote.

Commission
- Gives positive opinion of Parliament's amendments; or
- gives negative opinion of Parliament's amendments.

Conciliation Committee
- Comprising equal numbers of Council and Parliament.
- Approves a joint text.
- Fails to approve a joint text.

Council
- Begins deliberating.
- Takes feedback also from Economic and Social Committee and Committee of the Regions.
- Communicates a common position to Parliament.
- Council adopts measure on basis of common position
- The measure is not adopted.

- Measure is adopted by qualified majority vote if amendments accepted within three months.
- Measure is adopted if amendments approved by unanimous vote.

- If measure not adopted in either case then passed to:

Council and Parliament
- Measure adopted if approved by both (Council by qualified majority vote, Parliament by simple majority) otherwise not adopted.
- Measure not adopted.

The Ordinary Legislative Procedure (formerly the co-decision procedure)

3.3.2 The Ordinary Legislative Procedure (formerly the co-decision procedure)

1. The co-decision procedure was introduced by TEU and simplified by the Treaty of Amsterdam and use extended by Treaty of Nice. Now following ToL, as the Ordinary Legislative Procedure it is the main method of legislating.

2. It has given more power to Parliament, i.e. after Parliament proposing amendments, the Council must consider them and if they reject them then the act is not adopted, but final adoption of measure is still with the Council.

3. There is also the possibility of a 'Conciliation Committee' made up of equal representation from Council and Parliament if Council does not accept all amendments.

4. It replaced the co-operation procedure in relation to internal market measures, and applies also to, for example, environment, transport, consumer protection, culture.

5. Following ToL, Art 5(1) TEU requires a process of conferral to limit the competences of the EU to legislate in particular areas. Where the EU institutions are not granted competence in the Treaties then there may be shared competence with the Member States, or the EU may act to support, co-ordinate or supplement the actions of Member States.

6. EU institutions have exclusive competence over: the customs union, competition rules, monetary policy for Member States in the Euro zone, marine biology and fisheries policy and international agreements.

3.3.3 The Special Legislative Procedure

1. Following ToL Art 289 TFEU provides for legislation by a Special Legislative Procedure.

2. This involves special cases where the Treaties provide for secondary legislation either:
   - by Parliament with Council's involvement (must be adopted jointly); or
   - by Council with Parliament's participation (Council only needs to consult Parliament).

3. Examples are under Art 64(3) TFEU and Art 86(1) TFEU.

3.4 Non-binding secondary legislation

1. Art 288 introduces the concept of 'soft laws', referring specifically to recommendations and opinions, but adds: 'Recommendations and opinions have no binding force.'

2. While having no legal force, they can be issued on any matter dealt with in the Treaties, and may be persuasive, particularly politically and morally.

3. Since TEU increasing use has been made of soft laws, particularly within the social context.

4. A classic example is the Commission Code of Practice on Sexual Harassment:
   - while the Code is not binding it should not be ignored;
   - indeed it provides the UK definition of sexual harassment which otherwise would not exist, and has been applied (*Insitu Cleaning Co. v Heads* (1995)).

3.5 General principles of law

3.5.1 General

1. These are often unwritten principles (but not always, e.g. equality – Art 157, etc.).

2. These are generally developed by the ECJ, using as its authority the now repealed Art 220 EC – the general duty on the Court of Justice to ensure that community law is observed.

3. They are nevertheless binding on the institutions, the Member States and individual citizens.

4. General principles are a familiar concept to those states with a 'civil' Roman law tradition.

5. So they are in essentially a statement of values and basic standards that the court will use in interpretation.

6. They are broad enough to be generally acceptable as principle, but specific application can cause controversy.

7. Since much EU law is essentially administrative, some principles have derived from administrative law of France and Germany, but some has also derived from UK law.

3.5.2 Proportionality

1. This is now written into the TFEU at Art 42: 'Any action by the EU shall not go beyond what is necessary to achieve the objectives of this treaty.'

2. The means used must be proportionate to the end to be achieved.

3. It derives from a German principle, *verhaltnismassigkeit*.

4. First stated in the *International Handelgesselschaft Case 5/73*: 'No burdens should be placed on the citizens except to the extent that it is necessary to achieve the purpose.'

5. So, if the burden is too great the court can disapply the measure (see *Bela Muhler Bergman v Grows Farm 114/76* and *Watson (Lynne) and Alessandro Belmann 118/75*).

3.5.3 Equality

1. A general principle of equal treatment and non-discrimination.

2. Equal situations must always be treated equally unless there are objective justifications for doing otherwise.

3. By Art 18 TFEU: no discrimination on nationality.

4. Art 157 was original specific provision on gender discrimination on pay – now the Treaty includes the general aim of equality between men and women.

5. But the principle also obviously applies in internal organisation (*Sabbatini v Parliament 20/71*).

6. Equality now extended through various directives to include preventing discrimination on race, sexual orientation, disability, religion and belief, age, etc.

3.5.4 Legal certainty and procedural rights

1. The basic principle is that the law in its application must be predictable. So:
   - there should be no retroactive laws (*Société pour l'exploitation des sucres v Commission 88/76*);
   - there will be respect for acquired rights, which cannot later be withdrawn;

- a person is entitled to act according to legitimate expectations, i.e. as though the law still applies (*Commission v Council 81/72*);
- persons affected should be identifiable;
- language should be easily understood;
- a person is entitled to a fair hearing (*Transocean Marine Paint Association v The Commission 17/74*). Also found in some secondary legislation, e.g. Directive 64/221 derogations on free movement.

3.5.5 The protection of fundamental human rights

1. Now contained in Art 11 TFEU: 'shall respect fundamental rights guaranteed by the European Convention ... and from the constitutional traditions common to the Member States...'.

2. A number of propositions emerge from this:
   - *audi alteram partem* – fair hearings before imposition of a penalty (*Transocean Marine Paint*);
   - penalty must be based on a clear, unambiguous case;
   - no retroactive laws;
   - no one should be subjected to two penalties;
   - entitlement to legal assistance and representation;
   - a person is protected from self-incrimination, so no requirement to answer leading questions;
   - respect for private life and inviolability of premises (*X v Commission 404/92*).

3. It originates from the constitutions of certain Member States (*The International Handelgesselschaft Case 11/70*).

4. But the ECJ is prepared to recognise the significance of human rights (*Nold v The Commission 4/73*).

5. Although the EU is not a signatory to the European Convention of Human Rights it is possible to invoke Articles of the Convention (*R v Kirk 63/83*).

6. There is now also a Charter of Rights accepted at the Nice Summit.

3.5.6 Subsidiarity

1. There is some reference to subsidiarity in the founding Treaties – decisions should be taken as closely as possible to citizens affected by them.

2. It was incorporated in the EU Treaty as Art 5 by TEU at the UK's insistence: 'In areas which do not fall within its exclusive competence, the community shall take action, in accordance with the principle of subsidiarity, only if and in so far as the objectives of the proposed action cannot be sufficiently achieved by the Member States and can therefore, by reason of the scale or effects of the proposed action, be better achieved by the community.'

3. So there is a two-fold test – community action can only be justified if it serves an end which:
   - cannot be achieved satisfactorily at national level; and
   - can be achieved better at community level.

3.6 Case law of the ECJ

1. Unlike English law, continental 'civil' systems have no binding system of precedent, and the ECJ follows the same principles.

2. Any binding force in the judgment then rests on the principle of *res judicita*.

3. So, for future cases ECJ judgments act as moral rather than strictly legal authority, and in the strictest technical sense then the court's judgments are not a formal source of law.

4. However, there are a number of qualifying points:
   - the court will not depart from its own rulings on law without pressing reasons, and judgments, if studied, show remarkable consistency;
   - a ruling in a particular case has an inevitable impact beyond the case itself;
   - the *Cilfit* rules on Art 267 references prevent repetitious references seeking new rulings on the same principle of law;
   - the ECJ has proved over the years to be very proactive;
   - indeed, many of the most definitive principles of EC law have originated in the ECJ, e.g. direct effect, indirect effect, state liability, etc.

4

Enforcement of EU law

Art 258 infringement proceedings against Member States

- Usually brought by Commission as watchdog.
- Three clear purposes:
  (i) to ensure Member States comply with Treaties;
  (ii) to provide a procedure for dispute resolution;
  (iii) to provide means of clarifying law.
- Starts with mediation, then three formal stages:
  (i) notice of default;
  (ii) reasoned opinion;
  (iii) proceedings in ECJ.
- Penalties possible in Art 260.
- An action by another state possible under Art 259 (*France v UK*).

ENFORCEMENT (DIRECT ACTIONS)

Art 263 actions against institutions for abuse of power:

- Two major functions:
  (i) provides way of controlling legality of binding acts;
  (ii) gives legal protection to those subject to Community instruments adversely affected by illegal ones.
- Commission, Council, Member States are privileged claimants.
- Natural and legal persons gain *locus standi* for a decision addressed to them or a regulation or a decision addressed to another person of direct and individual concern to them or against a regulatory act of direct concern to them and not entailing implementing measures.
- Individual concern means decision affects them because of attributes (*Plaumann v Commission*).
- A Regulation may be challenged if it has no general application but is a 'bundle of individual Decisions' (*International Fruit Co. v Commission*).
- Grounds for review include: lack of competence, infringement of an essential procedural requirement, infringement of Treaties or procedural rules, misuse of powers.

Art 265 actions against institutions for failing to act:

- Can challenge Commission, Council, Parliament, European Central Bank.
- Privileged claimants are Member States and institutions.
- Natural and legal persons must show institution failed to address to them any instrument other than an opinion or recommendation.
- Grounds for review are where applicant can show he was entitled to a Decision and none was addressed to him, or an action has not been taken which is of direct and individual concern to him.

Art 340 actions for damages against institutions:

- 'To make good any damage caused by institutions.'
- Almost unrestricted *locus standi*.
- D must be an institution or its servant, not Community as a whole (*Werhahn Hansamuhle v Council*).
- Conditions for liability are:
  (i) damage suffered by claimant;
  (ii) fault of institution;
  (iii) causal connection.

4.1 Enforcement: introduction

1. Substantive rights and obligations granted under Treaties would be ineffective if left merely to the co-operation of Member States.

2. Individual rights may be abused by EU institutions and by Member States.

3. So, a variety of enforcement proceedings and methods for reviewing the actions of both institutions and Member States were created in the Treaty, placed under the scrutiny of the ECJ, with individuals able to gain remedies.

4. These procedures are known as 'direct actions' and supplement 'indirect actions' of Art 267 reference procedure.

5. The measures are broad in that they allow a wide range of applicants to initiate proceedings.

4.2 Art 258 infringement proceedings against Member States

4.2.1 Introduction

1. EU law depends on a partnership with Member States, e.g. in the implementation of directives.

2. But it is not uncommon for Member States to be careless or even reluctant in fulfilling their obligations.

3. So, the Treaty provides the means of calling Member States to account.

4. It is normally invoked by the Commission under Art 258.

5. But it can be initiated by other Member States under Art 259.

4.2.2 Actions by the Commission under Art 258

1. Commission is 'watchdog of Treaties' so is empowered by Art 258 to monitor behaviour of Member States and enforce compliance with Treaty obligations if necessary.

2. By Art 258: 'if Commission considers a member state has failed to fulfil an obligation … it shall deliver a reasoned opinion on the matter after giving state concerned opportunity to submit its observations. If state

concerned does not comply ... within period laid down [Commission] may bring matter before Court of Justice.'

3. So Art 258 has three clear purposes:
   - to ensure Member States comply with Treaty obligations;
   - to provide a procedure for dispute resolution;
   - to provide means of clarifying law for all Member States.
4. There are three formal stages in the procedure – but these are usually preceded by an informal stage.
   - Mediation (informal): the Commission engages in discussions with the Member State, which will usually remedy the error at this point. The action is then discontinued.
   - Formal notice of default:
     (i) where the Commission remains dissatisfied it issues a notice inviting the Member State to submit its own observations;
     (ii) this stage defines the terms of reference which are then fixed (*Commission v Italy (Re Payment of Export Rebates) 31/69*).
   - Reasoned opinion:
     (i) issued if the Member State still fails to comply;
     (ii) sets out reasons why the Member State is in default and a time limit;
     (iii) but is not itself binding (*Alfonse Lutticke GmbH v Hauptzollamt Saarlouis 57/65*).
   - Court proceedings in the ECJ:
     (i) the Commission brings an action if the Member State still fails to comply;
     (ii) but the issue can still be settled without a court decision, e.g. interim relief under Art 279;
     (iii) many defences have been tried, but most fail:
       a) internal difficulties (*Commission v Belgium 77/69*);
       b) reciprocity (*Commission v France (Re restrictions on lamb imports) 232/78*);
       c) *force majeure* (*Commission v Italy 101/84*);
       d) objections by trade unions (*Commission v UK 128/78*).
5. Enforcement:
   - before TEU the ECJ's decisions were incapable of actual enforcement, so more Art 258 proceedings were used;
   - now, by Art 260, a financial penalty is possible, e.g. *Commission v Greece C-387/97* and this would particularly apply where there is a serious breach of EU law (*Commission v France C-121/07*).

4.2.3 Actions brought by Member States under Art 259

1. This was always intended to be an exceptional procedure.

2. However, it is a useful safeguard against errors of judgment by the Commission.

3. It is a similar procedure, though the Member State should work closely with the Commission in preliminary stages.

4. Only one case has been brought so far – *France v UK 141/78*.

4.3 Art 263 actions against Institutions for exceeding powers

4.3.1 Introduction

1. Art 263 is one of the few instances by which individuals can bring action in the ECJ, though their ability to do so is more restricted than for Institutions.

2. The procedure has two major functions:
   - it provides a means of controlling the legality of binding acts of Community institutions;
   - it gives legal protection to those subject to Community instruments adversely affected by illegal ones.

4.3.2 *Locus standi*

1. Member States, the Commission and the Council are all named in Art 263.
   - So are all 'privileged claimants' with virtually unlimited rights of challenge (except for recommendations and opinions).
   - Provided the measure complained of has binding effect on the claimant.

2. Parliament and the European Central Bank are privileged claimants but with more limited powers of challenge. They may only bring an action 'for the purpose of protecting their prerogatives'.

3. Natural and legal persons also gain *locus standi* by Art 263, but rights of challenge are limited to 'a Decision addressed to that person, or a

Decision which, although in the form of a Regulation or a Decision addressed to another person, is of direct and individual concern to the individual or against a regulatory act of direct concern to them and not entailing implementing measures…'.

4. So, except in the case of decisions addressed to the individual, there are three key issues to be established:

■ What is individual concern?

   (i) The decision must affect the applicant 'by reason of certain attributes which are peculiar to them or by reason of circumstances in which they are differentiated from all other persons and by virtue of these factors distinguishes them individually just as … person addressed …' (*Plaumann v Commission 25/62*).

   (ii) Since modified to extent it must be possible to determine the identity of persons affected at the time the measure complained of was adopted (*Toepfler v Commission 106 and107/63*).

   (iii) The ECJ has said there must be a 'closed group' of people affected (*International Fruit Co. v Commission 41-44/70*).

   (iv) However, there is inconsistent application (*Piraiki-Patraiki v Commission 11/82*).

   (v) The AG in *UPA v Council C-50/00* suggested that a better test was 'has the individual suffered a substantial adverse affect?' – but ECJ confirmed *Plaumann* test in *Jego-Quere et cie v Commission T-177/01*.

■ What is direct concern?

   (i) It is different from individual concern, but still subject to inconsistent interpretation.

   (ii) As well as causal connection it refers to 'immediate, automatic and inevitable disadvantageous legal effects' without need for further intervention (*Alcan Aluminium Raeren et al v Commission 69/69*).

   (iii) However, this strict standard has since been relaxed (*Bock v Commission 62/70 (The Chinese Mushrooms Case)*).

   (iv) But direct concern involves affecting the legal situation of the person concerned, so members of political parties acting on their own behalf rather than the party's fail the test (*Bonde and Others v Parliament and Council T-13/04; Bonion and Others v Parliament and Council T-40/04; Front National and Others v Parliament and Council T-17/041*).

■ When is a Regulation to be seen as a 'Decision affecting the applicant'?
   (i) Genuine Regulations are never capable of challenge by an individual (*Calpak SpA v Commission 789/79*).
   (ii) So, a Regulation must fit the label given to it – *Confederation Nationale des Producteurs de Fruits et Legumes v Council 16 and 17/72*: 'what distinguishes a Regulation is not the greater or lesser extent of its application, material or territorial, but the fact that its provisions apply impersonally in objective situations …'.
   (iii) So, a Regulation may be challenged when it has no general application but is 'a bundle of individual Decisions taken by the Commission, each of which, although taken in the form of a Regulation, affected the legal position of the applicant …' (*International Fruit Co. v Commission 41-44/70*).

4.3.3 Substantive grounds for review

1. Once admissibility is established the claimant must show that the challenge concerns one of four grounds identified in Article.

2. Lack of competence:
   ■ there is no direct comparison in English law, but seen as comparable to the *ultra vires* doctrine;
   ■ it occurs if an institution exercises a power not conferred upon it by EU law, or exercises a non-existent power, or encroaches on the power of another institution;
   ■ the ECJ has defined the ground but will rarely accept challenges between institutions (*Commission v Council (Re European Road Transport Agreement) 22/70 (The ERTA case)*);
   ■ so, it is more likely to be used for powers not possessed at all (*Ford (Europe) v Commission 228 and 229/82*);
   ■ or often for improper delegation (*Meroni v High Authority 9/56*).

3. Infringement of an essential procedural requirement:
   ■ EU law imposes procedural requirements as safeguards.
   ■ Essential procedures include:
      (i) preparation, e.g. prior consultation (*Roquette Freres v Council 138/79*);
      (ii) communication giving reasons (*Germany v Commission 52 and 55/65*).

4. Infringement of Treaties or rules relating to their application:
   - allows the ECJ to review whether the acts of the institutions conform to EU law;
   - can include all aspects, e.g. general principles, so any sort of violation of EU law will be invalid (*Transocean Marine Paint Association v Commission 17/74*).

5. Misuse of powers:
   - refers to institution using a power it possesses but for objects contrary to those for which it was granted;
   - may include any illegitimate use of power (*Bock v Commission 62/70 (The Chinese Mushrooms case)*).

4.3.4 Procedure

1. The most important requirement is a strict time-limit for bringing an action.

2. This is two months from date on which the measure was published, was notified to the claimant or came to his attention – but this may be extended if there are unforeseeable circumstances or *force majeure*.

3. The consequences of a successful claim is for the instrument to be declared void by the ECJ.

4.4 Art 265 actions against Institutions for a failure to act

4.4.1 General

1. Art 265 allows Member States and Community institutions to challenge the Council, Commission, Parliament and European Central Bank for not acting when they should.

2. It is the natural corollary of Art 263 proceedings.

3. Applicants must satisfy admissibility and show suitable grounds for review.

4.4.2 Admissibility

1. Three conditions must be met.
2. Title to sue (*locus standi*):
   - 'privileged claimants' are 'Member States and other institutions', which now includes Parliament (*Parliament v Council 377/87*);
   - 'natural and legal persons' can bring action against an institution which failed to address to that person any instrument other than a recommendation or an opinion.
3. It must be an indictable institution – the Council, Commission, Parliament or the Central Bank.
4. A prior approach to the institution:
   - must be made by the applicant before applying to the ECJ;
   - it must be explicit and refer to the possibility of Art 265 if no reply within two months.

4.4.3 Grounds for review

1. Will be where the applicant can show he was entitled to a decision and none was addressed to him, or an action has not been taken which is of direct and individual concern to him.
2. Few cases are admissible so there are few guidelines.
3. Generally, if there is a result to be achieved and an obligation is sufficiently well defined then any attempt to disregard it will fall within scope of Art 265 (*Parliament v Council 13/83*).

4.5 Art 340 actions for damages

4.5.1 General

1. Art 340 states: 'In the case of non-contractual liability, the EU shall … make good any damage caused by the Institutions or by its servants in the performance of their duties'.
2. So, it is a general tort action but based more on French civil law.

4.5.2 Admissibility

1. *Locus standi* is almost unrestricted – any natural or legal person can claim provided the party him/herself has suffered damage resulting from an act or omission of an institution or its servant.

2. The defendant must be an institution or its servant, not the EU as a whole (*Werhahn Hansamuhle v Council 63-69/72*).

3. The appropriate time-limit is five years from the date of the event giving rise to the action.

4.5.3 Conditions for liability

1. Three elements must be satisfied for a successful claim.

2. Damage suffered by the claimant:
   - can be any damage that is certain, provable and quantifiable;
   - future loss is recoverable in some circumstances (*Kampffmeyer et al v Commission 5,7 and 13-24/66*);
   - even highly speculative loss is recoverable in some circumstances (*Adams v Commission 145/83*).

3. Fault on the part of the institution complained of:
   - it is only necessary to show that the claimant was owed a duty which was breached (*Adams v Commission 145/83*);
   - but the ECJ is less likely to conclude fault where the institution makes policy decisions and errs (*Zuckerfabrik Schoppenstedt v Council 5/71*);
   - although it has been established that liability is possible even in the absence of unlawful conduct (*FIAMM and FIAMM Technologies v Council and Commission T-69/00*) provided that there is unusual and special damage (*Galileo v Commission T-279/03*).

4. A causal connection between measure and damage:
   - proof of damage alone is insufficient for liability without proof that the act of the institution directly caused it (*Dumortier Frères SA v Council 27,28 and 45/79*);
   - so remoteness is an important factor (*Pool v Council 49/79*).

5

The relationship between EU law and national law

Supremacy:

- Vital to ensure supranational character of institutions, but not mentioned in Treaties.
- First stated in *Van Gend en Loos* – states have given up sovereignty to new legal order.
- Explained in *Costa v ENEL* – clear limitation of sovereign right upon which subsequent unilateral law, incompatible with aims of Community, cannot prevail.
- Any conflict is settled in favour of EU law (Simmenthal).
- Following *R v Secretary of State for Transport, ex parte Factortame No (2)* national court can do everything necessary to set aside national legislative provisions which might prevent Community (now EU) rules from having full force and effect.

EU LAW AND NATIONAL LAW

Art 267 References:

- Means of ensuring uniform applications of EU law.
- Any court may refer – some have mandatory referral.
- ECJ test in CILFIT of where reference unnecessary: where EU law irrelevant or peripheral; or where there is an existing interpretation; or where correct interpretation is so obvious that no doubt.
- *Fogilla v Novella*: reference must involve genuine issue of EU law; and will genuinely assist national court to make a judgment; but cannot be used merely to test the law or to delay the case.

Direct applicability

- Measure becomes part of national law without further enactment.
- So applies to Regulations but not to directives.

Direct effect:

- *Van Gend en Loos v Nederlands Administratie der Belastingin* accepted that certain measures should be enforceable by citizens of Member States – if they were clear, precise and unconditional, and conferred rights on individuals;
- this is straightforward in the case of substantive Treaty Articles – *Reyners v Belgium*;
- and even in the case of decisions – *Grad v Finanzamt Traustein*;
- but not for directives which are not a complete legal instrument.

Direct effect of directives:

- *Van Duyn v Home Office* recognised that it would be incompatible with the binding nature of a directive in Art 288 if they could not be enforced;
- so provided that the date for implementation is passed – *Pubblico Ministero v Ratti*;
- they may be 'vertically' directly effective against the state itself – *Marshall v Southampton and SW Hampshire AHA (No 1)*;
- or an 'emanation of the state' – *Foster v British Gas plc*.

Indirect effect:

- *Von Colson and Kamann v Land Nordrhein-Westfalen* allows that since Member States have an obligation formerly under Art 10 (now Art 4(3) TEU) to give full effect to EU law then they should interpret an improperly implemented directive so as to give effect to its objectives.

State liability:

- *Brasserie/Factortame* provides an action against states for failure to implement directives where the citizen suffers loss as a result.

5.1 Supremacy of EU law

5.1.1 The reasons for the doctrine of supremacy

1. Supremacy has become:
   - the most entrenched; and
   - probably the least contested of EU principles.

2. It is essential that EU law should be uniformly applied.

3. Without 'supremacy' there could be no supranational context for the institutions, which would then have no effective power.

4. So, the real justifications for supremacy are:
   - the prevention of any questioning of the validity of EU law in Member States.
   - the doctrine of 'pre-emption':
     - (i) prevention of alternative legal interpretations of EU law by Member State courts;
     - (ii) prevention of enactment of conflicting legislating by Member State governments.

5. However, the Treaties themselves make no reference to supremacy over all national law. The closest is the former Art 10 (the duty of loyalty) (now in Art 4(3) TEU): 'Member States shall take all appropriate measures … to ensure fulfillment of the obligations arising out of this Treaty or resulting from actions taken by the institutions … They shall abstain from any measure which could jeopardize the attainment of the objectives of the Treaty …'. This has become a major tool in the hands of the ECJ.

6. Ultimately, the most logical basis for supremacy is the requirement of full integration. In any case economic integration would be virtually impossible if Member States could deny and defy the supranational powers of the institutions.

5.1.2 The early statements of supremacy

1. The earliest definition of supremacy is in *26/62 Van Gend en Loos v The Commission*: 'The Community (now EU) constitutes a new legal order in international law, for whose benefits the states have limited their sovereign rights, albeit within limited fields …'.

2. The key effect of supremacy, then, is to limit the ability of Member States to legislate contrary to EU law.

3. The definitive explanation came in *6/64 Costa v ENEL*: 'By contrast with ordinary international treaties, the EEC Treaty has created its own legal system which on entry into force... became an integral part of the legal systems of the Member States and which their courts are bound to apply ... The transfer by Member States from their national orders in favour of the Community (now EU) order ... carries with it a clear limitation of their sovereign right upon which a subsequent unilateral law, incompatible with the aims of the Community cannot prevail ...'.

4. Three points clearly emerge:
   - Member States have given up certain of their sovereign powers to make law;
   - Member States and their citizens are bound by EU law;
   - Member States cannot unilaterally introduce conflicting law.

5. The ECJ has also declared that EU law cannot be invalidated even by national constitutional law – *International Handelsgesellschaft v EVGF 11/70*: 'Recourse to the legal rules or concepts of national law in order to judge the validity of measures adopted by the institutions ... would have an adverse effect on the uniformity and efficacy of EC (now EU) law. The validity of such measures can only be judged in the light of Community law...'.

6. So the ECJ has insisted that where EU law and national law conflict a court must give effect to the EU law – *Simmenthal SpA 106/77* 'the relationship between the provisions of the Treaty and directly applicable measures of the institutions on the one hand and national law ... on the other... render automatically inapplicable any conflicting provision of current national law but ... also preclude the valid adoption of new national legislative measures to the extent that they would be incompatible with Community (now EU) provisions ... every national court must ... apply Community (now EU) law in its entirety ... and must accordingly set aside any provision of national law which may conflict with it whether prior or subsequent ...'.

7. Supremacy applies not only to directly conflicting national law, but to any contradictory law which encroaches on an area of EU competence (*Commission v France (The Merchant Sailor's case) 167/63*).

5.1.3 Continued development of the doctrine

1. The ECJ has continued to modify and expand the principle.

2. Another far reaching statement allowed national courts to set aside national legislation in areas of conflict – *R v Secretary of State for Transport, ex parte Factortame No (2) C-213/89*: 'any legislative, administrative, or judicial practice which might impair the effectiveness of Community law (now EU) by withholding from the national court … the power to do everything necessary … to set aside national legislative provisions which might prevent … Community (now EU) rules from having full force and effect are incompatible with those requirements which are the very essence of Community (now EU) law … the full effectiveness of Community (now EU) law would be just as much impaired if a rule of national law could prevent a court … from granting interim relief… It therefore follows that a court which … would grant interim relief, if it were not for a rule of national law, is obliged to set aside that law…'.

3. The ECJ has also developed the principle that courts must interpret national legislation to comply with EU obligations, whether national law precedes or follows the conflicting EU law (*Von Colson v Land Nordrhein-Westfalen 14/83*, further developed by *Marleasing v La Comercial 106/89*).

4. The principle of liability towards citizens who suffer loss from a Member State's breach of EU law also extends the doctrine of supremacy (*Francovich v Italy 6/90 and 9/90*).

5.1.4 Responses to supremacy by Member States

1. Different states have responded in different ways.

2. Belgium and supremacy:
   - a monist state in respect of the international Treaty;
   - but EU law was incorporated by statute, so some early doubts on supremacy;
   - issue settled in *Minister for Economic Affairs v Fromagerie Franco-Suisse 'Le Ski'* (1972) – usual rule that a later statute repeals an earlier one could not apply to EU law, so EU law was supreme.

3. France and supremacy:
   - differences have occurred between civil appeal court views and administrative court (*Conseil d'Etat*);

- civil courts have always accepted that EU law prevails over inconsistent cases and statute (*Von Kempis v Geldof* (1976));
- but *Conseil d'Etat* has held that Directives cannot be used to challenge national administrative law (*Minister for the Interior v Cohn Bendit* (1975));
- though recently more prone to accept the principle.

4. Italy and supremacy:
   - takes a 'constructionist' approach – Italian law construed to be consistent with EU law;
   - the leading case is *Frontini* (1974): EU law is separate and superior and not within the scope of review of the Italian constitutional court.

5. Germany and supremacy:
   - originally favoured constitution over EU because of human rights (*International Handelsgesselschaft* (1970))
   - but supremacy accepted if human rights were upheld (*Wunsche Handelsgesselschaft* (1987))
   - but is still prone to argue for national sovereignty (*Brunner* (1994)).

6. UK and supremacy:
   - In the UK the focus has always been on interpretation of the EC Act 1972.
   - Section 2(1) gives force to EU law: 'All such rights, powers, liabilities, obligations and restrictions… created or arising by or under the Treaties, are without further enactment to be given legal effect …'.
   - Supremacy appears to be guaranteed by s 2(4) which provides: '… any enactment passed or to be passed … shall be construed and have effect subject to the foregoing provision of this section …'.
   - Traditional argument has centred on whether it is an entrenched principle or merely a rule of construction.
   - Judges have been willingly liberal in taking the latter view (*Garland v British Rail Engineering Ltd* (1979)).
   - Judges have advocated a purposive approach to interpretation (*Pickstone v Freeman* (1988) and *Litster v Forth Dry Dock Co.* (1989)).
   - However, in *Duke v Reliance GEC* (1988) Lord Templeman suggested that s 2(4) does not permit an English court to 'distort a statute to enforce a Directive which has no direct effect between individuals…'.
   - On Parliament's ability to deliberately oppose the EU, Lord Denning's view was: 'if…Parliament deliberately passes an Act with

the intention of repudiating the Treaty or any provisions in it ... and says so in express terms, then I would have thought that it would be the duty of our courts to follow the statute of our Parliament...' (*Macarthys v Smith 129/79*) – so ECA 1972 cannot be impliedly repealed though express repeal is theoretically retained.

■ But acceptance of supremacy is now more clearly stated – Hoffman J in *Stoke-on-Trent v B and Q plc* (1990): 'The EC Treaty is the supreme law of the UK taking precedence over Acts of Parliament. Entry into the EU meant that Parliament surrendered its sovereign right to legislate contrary to the provisions of the Treaty ... partial surrender of sovereignty was more than compensated for by the advantages of membership...'.

■ And the definitive view of the meaning and scope of the 1972 Act is now Lord Bridge's in *Factortame*: '... whatever limitations of its sovereignty Parliament accepted when it enacted the EC Act 1972 was entirely voluntary. Under the terms of the 1972 Act it has always been clear that it is the duty of a UK court, when delivering final judgement, to override any rule of national law found to be in conflict with any directly enforceable rule of Community (now EU) law...'.

5.2 Direct applicability and direct effect

5.2.1 Introduction

1. With supremacy, direct effect is another major element in ensuring the application of EU law in the Member States.

2. It must be distinguished from direct applicability – Art 288 refers to certain community measures being either generally applicable or directly applicable.

3. The three are distinguished as follows:
   ■ general applicability merely means that the measure applies throughout the whole EU (so it would apply to a regulation but not to a decision);
   ■ direct applicability means that the measure becomes part of national law without need for further enactment (so it would apply to a regulation but not to a directive);
   ■ direct effect means that the measure creates rights and obligations which are enforceable in the national courts as well as in the ECJ (so

it could easily apply to Treaty Articles and regulations, but is more problematic when applied to directives).

4. So there is a distinction between these last two:
   - directly applicable measures need not create justiciable rights e.g. a procedural regulation;
   - direct effect can exist without direct applicability, e.g. a Directive;
   - but a measure could be both.

5. Direct effect has been described as 'the first step in the judicial contribution to federalism…' (Craig: *Once upon a time in the west*).

6. It has also been described as 'a second principle of western jurisprudence to run alongside supremacy; namely the rule of law…' (Ian Ward: *A critical introduction to European law*).

7. Its most powerful justification is that it 'enhances the effectiveness or effet utile of binding norms of Community (now EU) law …' (Josephine Shaw: *Law of the European Union*, Palgrave).

8. It is the creation of the ECJ – its uncompromising nature has resulted in conflict with Member States and in turn even more uncompromising principles, such as indirect effect.

5.2.2 The basic requirements for direct effect

1. The principle was first accepted by the ECJ in *Van Gend en Loos v Nederlands Administratie der Belastingen 26/62*: 'Community (now EU) law … not only imposes obligations on individuals but is also intended to confer upon them rights which become part of their legal heritage. These rights are granted not only where they are expressly granted by the Treaty, but also by reason of obligations which the Treaty imposes in a clearly defined way upon individuals as well as upon Member States and the institutions of the Community (now EU) …'.

2. So the ECJ accepted that since the Treaty was clearly intended to affect individuals as well as Member States, it must be capable of creating rights which were enforceable by individuals.

3. The ECJ held that since Art 25 (now Art 30 TFEU) 'contains a clear and unconditional prohibition … it [is] ideally adapted to produce direct effects between Member States and their subjects …'.

4. By *Van Gend en Loos* direct effect only applied to 'stand still Articles':
   - but this limitation soon disappeared;
   - and a variety of provisions have since been held to be directly effective;

- though there are still measures which remain unenforceable if worded in conditional terms.

5. The requirements for direct effect have been modified by the case law, e.g. *Reyner v Belgium 2/74* and are: the provision must be clear, precise and unconditional and non-dependent.

6. *Van Gend en Loos* concerned a Treaty Article that conferred rights, but the principle of direct effect has been extended to other EU law by the case law.

5.2.3 The basic distinction between vertical and horizontal direct effect

1. The ECJ has also been responsible for helping to identify the principles of vertical and horizontal direct effect and clarifying the distinctions between them.

The differences between vertical and horizontal direct effect

2. The distinction can be critical in determining whether a person can enforce EU law in a national court.

3. Vertical direct effect concerns the relationship between EU law and the national law:
   - measures of EU law create obligations on the state;
   - so failure to honour such obligations would normally result in Art 258 action;
   - but it can also mean that an individual can rely on the measures in an action against the state;
   - this was the case in both *Van Duyn v Home Office 41/74* and *Pubblico Ministero v Ratti 148/78*, which were both fought against government departments;
   - the concept has been extended to include bodies that are 'emanations of the state' (public bodies) and so may extend rights to certain individuals.

4. Horizontal direct effect, on the other hand, is precisely about the relationship between individuals, so concerns rights enforceable in national courts.

5.2.4 Direct effect and Treaty articles

1. Direct effect was first accepted in *Van Gend en Loos*.

2. However, the principal test for application now is that laid down in *Reyners v Belgium 2/74*.

3. Directly effective Treaty Articles could include:
   - 'stand still' Articles, e.g. *Van Gend en Loos* and Art 25 (now Art 30 TFEU);
   - originally also included Articles imposing a duty on the state to act, e.g. *Eunomia 18/71* on Art 16 (now repealed);
   - Articles that give rights to individuals, e.g. *Van Duyn v Home Office 41/74* and Art 45; *Reyners v Belgium 2/74* and Art 49; *Defrenne v SABENA 43/75* and Art 157.

5.2.5 Direct effect and Regulations

1. Regulations create obligations without need for further enactment because they are of 'general application' and are 'directly applicable'.

2. So they will usually be directly effective, subject to *Reyners* test (*Leonesio v Ministero dell'Agricoltora and delle Foreste 93/71 (The widow Leonesio)*).

3. But a Regulation may not be directly effective if too vague.

5.2.6 Direct effect and Decisions

1. A decision by Art 288 is 'binding in its entirety on the party to whom it is addressed'.

2. So it would be 'incompatible with the binding nature of decisions to exclude the possibility of direct effect...' (*Grad v Finanzamt Traustein 9/70*).

3. It is less certain whether a decision addressed to a Member State could have horizontal effect.

5.2.7 Direct effect and Directives

1. By Art 288, directives are 'binding as to the result to be achieved':
   - so they are seen as creating an obligation on Member States to pass law to achieve the objective;
   - but not as automatically creating substantive rights for citizens to enforce, because they fail the *Van Gend* test – they are dependent.

2. The ECJ was prepared to overlook this limitation in *Van Duyn v Home Office*:
   - because 'it would be incompatible with the binding effect attributed to a Directive by (Art 288) to exclude, in principle, the possibility that the obligation which it imposes may be invoked by those concerned ...';
   - so a directive can be enforced provided that the three criteria for direct effect are met.

3. But only where the time-limit for implementation has passed (*Pubblico Ministero v Ratti 148/78*).

4. Also, a directive can be vertically but not horizontally effective (*Marshall v Southampton and South West Hampshire AHA (Teaching) (No 1) 152/84*).

5. Where the directive is properly implemented there would be national law and so need to use direct effect. An unimplemented directive can only be relied on as against the state, e.g.:

- pre-privatised British Gas (*Foster v British Gas plc 188/89*); tax authorities (*Becker 8/81*); and the police (*Johnston v The Royal Ulster Constabulary 222/84*);
- but not a publicly owned manufacturing company (*Rolls Royce plc v Doughty* (1987));
- the test in *Foster* and also in *Griffin v South West Water* (1995) is whether:
  - (i) the body provides a public service;
  - (ii) the body is under the control of the state;
  - (iii) the body exercises special powers;
- so this creates major anomalies in the case of private bodies (*Duke v Reliance GCE* (1988)), against whom an unimplemented directive cannot be enforced.

6. A directive can be referred to after implementation to ensure its objectives are achieved *Verbond v Nederlands Ondernemingen 51/76*.

5.2.8 Indirect effect

1. As a result of the limitations of using vertical direct effect, the ECJ has used the obligation under the former Art 10 (now Art 4(3) TEU) to conform with and give effect to EU law (irrespective of whether or not it is directly effective) to develop the principle of indirect effect (the *Von Colson* principle), which applies to all EU law, not just directives.

2. As the court said in *Von Colson and Kamann v Land Nordrhein-Westfalen 14/83*, 'Since the duty under [Art 10] (now Art 4(3) TEU) to ensure fulfillment of (an) obligation was binding on all national courts ... it follows that ... courts are required to interpret their national law in the light of the wording and purpose of the directive ...'.

3. The ECJ in *Von Colson* ignored the horizontal/vertical issue, and direct effect generally:
   - it was left ambiguous to which national law indirect effect would apply so, for example, HL refused to apply it in *Duke*;
   - it was also left ambiguous how far national courts should go to ensure conformity of national law and EU law.

4. However, these problems seem to have been resolved by *Marleasing SA v La Comercial Internacional de Alimentacion C-106/89*:
   - the ECJ held that the obligation to conform applied 'whether the provisions concerned pre-date or post-date the directive ...';

- so its scope in *Marleasing* is potentially very wide, with consequences for precedent and statutory interpretation;
- although there does seem to be a difference between the *Von Colson* approach (to do 'everything possible' to achieve conformity), and the *Simmenthal* approach (to do 'everything necessary');
- the ECJ already seems to have linked the concepts of direct and indirect effect (*Johnston v Chief Constable of the RUC 222/84*).

5.2.9 State liability for failure to implement

1. The third way to avoid the problems of direct effect and directives came in *Francovich v Italy 6/90 and 9/90*:
   - the ECJ held that 'the full effectiveness of EC (now EU) provisions ... and the rights they recognise would be undermined if individuals were unable to recover damages where their rights were infringed by a breach of EC (now EU) law attributable to a member state ...';
   - so citizens should be able to sue the state for non-implementation of a directive.

2. The conditions for liability are:
   - the directive must confer rights for individuals – the contents of which must be identifiable in the wording;
   - there must be a causal link between the damage suffered and the failure to implement the directive;
   - and the cases of *Brasserie du Pêcheur SA v Germany* and *R v Secretary of State for Transport, ex parte Factortame 46 and 48/93* have added another – that the breach by the Member State is sufficiently serious;
   - *Dillenkofer v Federal Republic of Germany C-178/94* suggests that non-implementation is sufficiently serious so this is like strict liability;
   - for other breaches, must show breach was sufficiently serious (*R v Minister of Agriculture, Fisheries and Food ex parte Hedley Lomas C-5/94*).

3. The *Francovich* principle is the most far reaching so far and has several implications:
   - it conflicts with national rules on non-implementation;
   - but the need to show direct effect is removed;
   - as is the strained construction of national law through indirect effect;
   - it focuses instead on the duty of the Member State to implement EU law and attaches rigorous sanctions for failure to implement;
   - so it removes any advantage of non-implementation.

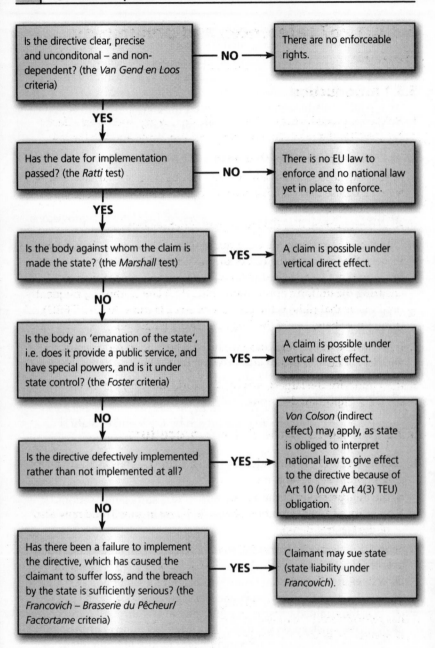

The possible enforceability of directives

5.3 Art 267 references and preliminary rulings

5.3.1 Introduction

1. Reference procedure is critical to both supremacy and direct effect, because it is the means of ensuring uniform application of the law.

2. The ethos of reference procedure is:
   - to create a collaborative bond between EU and the national courts;
   - to recognise that national courts are ultimately the best equipped to give effect to EU law;
   - to demonstrate that EU law is part of national law.

3. 'The grand objectives of a Community (now EU) legal order which include the intermeshing of Community (now EU) law and national law, could not be achieved without some organic mechanism for ensuring the uniform application of EC (EU) law … the ECJ frequently reminds us that (this) is the purpose of Art 234 (now Art 267 TFEU) …'. (Josephine Shaw, *Law of the European Union*, Palgrave)

4. It provides a means for national courts to be guided on 'meaning or validity' of EU law in a case depending on EU law.

5. It accounts for the largest area of ECJ work, and for most of the crucially important decisions.

5.3.2 The scope of the Art 267 procedure

1. Under Art 267(1), as amended by the TEU, the ECJ has jurisdiction to give preliminary rulings on:
   - the interpretation of the TFEU;
   - validity and interpretation of acts of EU institutions (and now also of the Central Bank).

2. So the ECJ clearly has jurisdiction to interpret all Treaty Articles and the acts of the institutions, which are clearly those in Art 288: Regulations, Directives and Decisions.

3. The ECJ has no jurisdiction to interpret national law. But sometimes has reformulated the question to better assist the national court (*Marks & Spencer v Customs and Excise Commissioners C-62/00*).

4. By Art 267(2), 'Where such a question is raised before any court or tribunal of a member state… [it] may, if it considers a decision on the question is necessary to enable it to give judgement, request the Court of Justice to give a ruling…'.

5. By Art 267(3), 'Where any such question is raised in a case pending before a court or tribunal of a member state, against whose decisions there is no judicial remedy under national law, that court or tribunal shall bring the matter before the Court of Justice'.

5.3.3 The meaning of 'any court or tribunal'

1. This may include 'the whole range of bodies which embody the judicial power of the state regardless of what they are called…'.

2. The key elements according to the ECJ in *Dorsch Consult C-54/96* are that the body:
   - must be recognised in the national judicial system;
   - must be a permanent body;
   - must exercise a judicial function;
   - must give a decision according to the rule of law.

3. Examples of bodies falling within Art 267 procedure include:
   - *Vaassen 61/65*, a Dutch Social Security Tribunal for migrant workers;
   - *Broeckmeuler 246/80*, a Dutch GP's Registration Appeals Committee;
   - *Pretore di Salo v X 14/86*, preliminary enquiries by a Magistrate;
   - *Abrahamsson v Andersson C-407/98*, the Swedish Universities Appeal Board;
   - *Korhonen C-18/01*, the Finnish Competition Council;
   - in the UK it has included Employment Tribunals, the EAT and Social Security Tribunals and more recently a Special Commissioners of Income Tax (*Cadbury Schweppes C-196/04*).

4. Examples of bodies not within the scope of Art 267 include:
   - *Borker 138/80*, the Paris Bar Council;
   - *Nordsee Hochseefischerei GmbH v Reederei Mond 102/81* and *Denuit & Cordenier C-125/04*, commercial arbitration;
   - *Saltzman C-78/99*, a District Court acting as a Land Registry;
   - *Lutz C-182/00*, a Regional Court acting as a Companies Registry.

5.3.4 Paragraph 2 and the discretion to refer

1. Paragraph 2 and paragraph 3 identify two different situations:
   - discretionary referral – from the word 'may' in 2;
   - mandatory referral – from the word 'shall' in 3.

2. By paragraph 2 courts have discretion to refer where they feel it is 'necessary'.

3. A national court will find it necessary when it requires an ECJ ruling in order to be able to give judgment.

4. The ECJ has developed its own test, in *CILFIT 283/81*, of when a reference is not necessary:

   ■ where EU law is irrelevant or peripheral to the issue;
   ■ where there is an existing interpretation – the principle of *acte clair* applies (see *Procureur de la Republique v Chiron 271/84* and *274/81*);
   ■ where correct interpretation is so obvious that there can be no doubt.

5. UK courts have also drawn up their own guidelines:

   ■ Lord Denning in *Bulmer v Bollinger* (1974) – before referring, judge must be sure:
      (i) EU law would be conclusive of the case;
      (ii) there is no previous ECJ ruling;
      (iii) the doctrine of *acte clair* does not apply;
      (iv) the facts of the case are already decided;
      (v) delay caused by reference is not unwarranted.

   ■ though these guidelines have been criticised for being too negative. A more positive approach is Bingham J in *Commissioners of Customs and Excise v Samex SpA* (1983) – the ECJ is better to interpret EU law because:
      (i) it scrutinises all the language versions;
      (ii) it oversees EU law in total;
      (iii) it has a better understanding of purposive interpretation.

5.3.5 Paragraph 3 and the obligation to refer

1. This is known as the 'compulsory reference' procedure – strangely as there is much controversy surrounding when it will apply.

2. One view is that only courts of last resort are covered, e.g. Supreme Court in the UK.

3. But another view is that it includes any court where the right to appeal is denied for whatever reasons, e.g. in *Costa v ENEL* the reference was made by a *guidice concilliatore* (an Italian Magistrate).

4. The position is very unsettled in the UK courts, e.g. see CA and *R v Henn and Darby* (1978) and the High Court, and *Magnavision NV v General Optical Council (No 2)* (1987).

5. In general the risk of the 'floodgates' being opened seems to suggest that the strict meaning of paragraph 3 is compromised for the *CILFIT* criteria.

6. However, failure by a court of last resort to refer can result in an Art 258 action against the Member State.

5.3.6 The limitations on making references

1. These were stated in *Foglia v Novella (No 1) 104/79 and (No 2) 244/80*:
   - reference must involve a genuine issue of EU law;
   - reference will genuinely assist a national court to make a judgment;
   - reference may not be used to give opinions on hypothetical situations in order to merely test the law;
   - nor can a party merely use it as a delaying tactic;
   - in these last two situations a reference will be refused.

2. The reference must be 'necessary'.

3. Only the ECJ has authority to declare provisions of EU law invalid – to prevent damaging uniform application of EU law *Firma Foto-Frost v Hauptzollampt Lubeck 314/85*.
   - So where question is on validity of secondary legislation, reference must be made *R (on application of BAT) v Secretary of State for Health C-491/01*.

5.3.7 The effect of preliminary ruling under Art 267

1. There is nothing specific in the Treaty to indicate what the effect will be.

2. However, it is clear that Member State courts are bound to decide cases in accordance with ECJ case law.

3. The ECJ has its own case law on the subject, suggesting that in a case where a reference has been made the ruling is binding on the national court (*Milch-Fett-und Eierkontor v HZA Saarbrucker 29/68*) (but English High Court refused to apply preliminary ruling in *Arsenal FC v Reed C-206/01*, although was reversed by CA).

4. Though it is the interpretation of law which is binding – there is no question of *res judicita* applying.

6

Introduction to the law of the internal market

6.1 The aims of the single market

1. The internal market is a system of regional economic and social integration – a large trading unit in which there are no internal barriers to trade.

2. The internal market also aims towards monetary unity and political integration that will secure not only the economic welfare of the citizens of European states, but will also secure peace.

3. Since enlargement in 2004, EU (by population) is the largest single trading bloc in the world.

6.2 The four freedoms

1. The logic of the founding Treaties was to create a single market, removing trade barriers based on national discrimination.

2. Hence the four freedoms identified in Art 26:
   - free movement of workers;
   - freedom to provide services;
   - free movement of capital;
   - free movement of goods.

3. Social mobility is ensured through Art 45 for workers, Art 49 for businesses or professions and Art 56 for providing services.

4. The purpose is to ensure that Member States do nothing to unfairly favour national enterprises and discriminate.

5. Free movement of goods is achieved in numerous ways:
   - by prohibiting customs duties on imports and exports, and all other charges having equivalent effect (Art 30);
   - by prohibiting discriminatory taxation (Art 110);

- by prohibiting quantitative restrictions (quotas) on imports and measures having equivalent effect (Art 34) and on exports (Art 35); exemptions exist in Art 36.

6. A Common Customs Tariff in Art 28 is governed by Art 31 and Art 32.

7. Goods are not defined in the Treaty, but have been defined as 'anything capable of money valuation and of being the object of commercial transactions ...' (*Commission v Italy Re Export Tax on Art Treasures 7/68*).

8. Economic Monetary Union (EMU) is also a necessary development towards creating a truly internal market:

- so EU has moved towards a single currency;
- but problematic because of relative economic stability of different states;
- so 'convergence criteria' created;
- many but not all states now use the single currency (not UK).

7

Art 34 and Art 35 and the free movements of goods

Prohibitions on quantitative restrictions – Art 34 and imports:

- Not defined in Treaty but is in case law – measures that amount to a total or partial restraint on imports, exports or goods in transit.
- So could include quota (*Salgoil SpA v Italian Minister of Trade*) or a complete ban on imports (*R v Henn & Darby*).
- Prohibited by Art 34.

Art 34 and exports:

- ECJ takes a different approach.
- Art 35 only restricts measures meant to differentiate between domestic and export trade and help exports at expense of other states (*Groenveld BV v Produktschap voor Veer en Vlees*).

Measures having equivalent effect (MEQRs):

- Not defined in Treaty, but in *Procureur du Roi v Dassonville* – all trading rules enacted by Member States which are capable of hindering, directly or indirectly, actually or potentially, intra-Community trade are to be considered as measures having an effect equivalent to quantitative restrictions – and are prohibited.
- But must distinguish between distinctly applicable (affects only imports) and indistinctly applicable (applies to imports and domestic goods – but affects imports disproportionately).
- But does not apply to selling arrangements if equally applied to imports and domestic goods (*Keck and Mithouard*).

FREE MOVEMENT OF GOODS

Cassis de Dijon principle:

- Principle in (*Cassis de Dijon case*) *Rewe-Zentral AG v Bundesmonopolverwaltung fur Branntwein*.
- Only applies to indistinctly applicable measures.
- Restriction lawful if to satisfy mandatory requirements for effective tax, protection of public health, fairness of commercial transactions or consumer protection – and proportionate.
- Second test – if product lawfully produced and marketed in one Member State then should be able to circulate freely throughout Community.

Art 36 derogations:

- Exemptions possible for public morality, public policy, or public security; protection of health of humans, animals or plants; protection of industrial and commercial property.
- List is exhaustive and narrower than *Cassis*.
- Art 36 can only be used if the measure is proportionate to the objective to be achieved, and non-arbitrary.
- Can only apply Art 36 to extent measure concerned is necessary to achieve objective – no further.
- Public morality varies by state (*R v Henn and Darby*).
- Public security only appropriate in crisis (*Campus Oil*).
- Public health must involve real risk to health (*Commission v UK (French Turkeys)*).

7.1 Prohibitions on quantitative restrictions on imports (Art 34), and exports (Art 35), and measures having equivalent effect

1. A quantitative restriction is a national measure that restricts the volume or amount of imports or exports, not by artificially raising the costs of importing or exports (as would be the case with a tariff or a tax), but by placing direct or indirect limits on the physical quantity of imports or exports that may enter or leave the market.

2. The Treaty deals with quantitative restrictions in:
   - Art 34 in the case of imports;
   - Art 35 in the case of exports;
   - Art 36 which provides exemptions from the prohibitions if certain justifications are shown.

3. Quantitative restrictions are not defined in the Treaty:
   - but they are in the case law: 'measures which amount to a total or partial restraint on imports, exports or goods in transit …' the (*Geddo v Ente Nazionale Rist* 2/73);
   - usually involves acts but can also be an omission (*Schmidberger v Austria* C-112/00);
   - the most common form of QR is quotas (*Salgoil SpA v Italian Minister of Trade* 13/68);
   - but can also include outright bans, e.g. a ban on importing pornographic material (*R v Henn & Darby* 34/79). And the Court of Justice has held that it also includes where a private individual is prohibited from importing alcoholic beverages (*Klas Rosengren and Others v Riksaklagaren* C-170/04).

7.2 Measures having equivalent effect (MEQRS)

1. 'Measures having equivalent effect to a quantitative restriction' (MEQR) are not defined in the Treaty, but have been widely interpreted (*Commission v Ireland (Re discriminatory promotional policies)* 249/81).

2. Directive 70/50 (subsequently repealed) identified MEQRs as:
   - distinctly applicable measures – those that apply only to imported goods and which make importing goods more difficult than using domestic products;
   - indistinctly applicable measures – those that are equally applicable to imported and domestic goods, which only contravene Art 34 if their restrictive effect exceeds the effect intrinsic to trade rules.

3. Practices identified under the Directive have included:
   - measures designed to specify less favourable prices for imports than for domestic products;
   - practices establishing minimum and maximum prices below or above which imports are prohibited or reduced;
   - standards subjecting imports to conditions relating to shape, size, weight or composition which cause them to suffer in competition with domestic products;
   - laws restricting marketing of imported products in the absence of an agent/representative in the importing state.

4. But definition is in the *Dassonville* formula: 'All trading rules enacted by Member States which are capable of hindering, directly or indirectly, actually or potentially, intra-Community trade are to be considered as measures having an effect equivalent to quantitative restrictions …' (*Procureur du Roi v Dassonville 8/74*).

5. Distinctly applicable MEQRs have included:
   - promoting domestic products (*Commission v Ireland (Buy Irish) 249/81*);
   - import licence requirements (*International Fruit 51 and 54/71*);
   - hygiene inspection for imports only (*Commission v UK (Re UHT Milk) 124/81*);
   - and might even include a failure to ban a demonstration that closed a major transit route for 30 hours (*Schmidberger C-112/00*).

6. Indistinctly applicable MEQRs have included:
   - origin marking (*Commission v UK 207/83*), and *Dassonville* was similar in requiring a certificate of origin;
   - packaging requirements (*Walter Rau v De Smedt 261/81*) (Belgian requirement for margarine to be in cube-shaped packages);
   - controls on ingredients (*Cassis de Dijon 120/78*), and *Commission v Germany (the Beer Purity case) 178/84*.

7.3 Art 36 and the derogations from Art 34 and Art 35

1. Art 36 provides derogations where 'justified on grounds of public morality, public policy, or public security; the protection of health and life of humans, animals or plants; the protection of national treasures possessing artistic, historic or archaeological value; or the protection of industrial and commercial property ... prohibitions and restrictions shall not, however, constitute a means of arbitrary discrimination or a disguised restriction on trade between Member States ...'.

2. So four key points stand out:
   - list is also exhaustive (and narrower than *Cassis*);
   - as a result, Art 36 must be construed strictly and narrowly;
   - Member States may claim exemptions under Art 36 only to the extent that the measure concerned is justified (necessary) to achieve the objective, and no further;
   - Art 36 only applies to QRs and distinctly applicable MEQRs (which are both direct discrimination).

3. So, inevitably situations arise where the ECJ will not apply Art 36 (*Commission v Ireland 113/80*).

4. The ECJ has struggled to produce a truly EU interpretation of public morality since moral perceptions vary from state to state (*R v Henn and Darby 34/79*).

5. Cases where public morality was used as an Art 36 derogation include *Conegate Ltd v Customs and Excise Commissioners 121/85* and *Quietlynn v Southend BC C-23/89* which show that there must be a genuine issue of morality which is applicable to domestic goods also.

6. On public policy too, the ECJ has interpreted strictly but without achieving a Community concept (*Commission v Germany 12/74 (the Sekt case)*), and the ground has only been successfully used once (*R v Thompson and Others 7/78*).

7. Public security is only likely to be successfully claimed in relation to a crisis (*Campus Oil 72/83*).

8. Protecting the health and life of humans, animals and plants is a straightforward public health exception:
   - The range of measures where a breach of Art 34 may occur includes: import bans, licensing systems, inspections (particularly

cross-border), prior authorisations, etc., any of which might be considered to be MEQRs (*Commission v UK (UHT Milk) 124/81*).

- But a real risk to health must be involved (*Commission v UK (French Turkeys) 40/82*).
- Art 36 can only apply if the measures are proportionate to the objectives to be achieved and protection of health cannot be achieved by other measures (*Commission v France (Re Italian Table Wines) 42/82*, but see also *Officier Van Justitie v Sandoz BV 174/82*, where a prohibition on an additive was allowed because there was no general medical consensus). ECJ in *Greenham and Abel C-95/01* laid down guidelines on the use of the health derogation for food additives – Member State need not wait for absolute proof of risk but must not base decision on purely hypothetical grounds.
- The real problem is the subjective character of analysing the real reasons for the restriction (*R v Secretary of State for the Home Department, ex parte Evans Medical and Macfarlane Smith C-324/93*).
- Failure of other states to operate according to recommendations but complying with a directive will not allow a state to rely on Art 36 (*R v Minister of Agriculture Fisheries and Food, ex parte Compassion in World Farming Ltd C-1/96* (19th March 1998)).

9. Protection of national treasures is a very precise area of justification, not yet successfully argued (*Commission v Italy (Re Export Tax on Art Treasures) 7/68*).

10. Protection of industrial and commercial property is, in effect, the intellectual property law of the EU and a giant area in its own right but property rights are difficult to define even in relation to a patent (*Centrafarm v Winthrop BV 15 and 16/74*).

11. But Art 36 has been used as a defence against national regulatory rules (*Torfaen BC v B and Q plc 145/88*).

7.4 The *Cassis de Dijon* principle

1. The wide scope of *Dassonville* meant that much indistinctly applicable national consumer protection legislation could breach Art 34 but was incapable of justification unless the health exemption could be used and ECJ interprets Art 36 strictly and narrowly.

2. As a result ECJ created the *Cassis de Dijon* rule of reason to allow Member States to plead a non-exhaustive list of 'mandatory requirements' including '*the effectiveness of fiscal provision, the protection*

of public health, the fairness of consumer transactions, and the defence of the consumer' as justifications for possible breaches, (*Rewe -Zentral AG v Bundesmonopolverwaltung fur Branntwein 120/78 (Cassis de Dijon case*)).

3. *Cassis* only applies to indistinctly applicable MEQRs which on the face of it are not discriminatory but could include a disguised discrimination:

   ■ so the rule of reason allows the court to determine which the measure is;
   ■ and only applies where the measure is necessary (*Familapress C-368/95*) and proportionate (*Clinique Laboratories C-315/92*);
   ■ unlike Art 36 the list of exemptions is not fixed so has expanded to include, e.g., consumer protection (*Commission v Germany 178/84*), the improvement of working conditions (*Oebel 155/80*), the protection of the environment (*Commission v Danmark (the Danish Bottles case 302/86*) and *Commission v Austria C-320/03*), protection of human rights (*Schmidberger v Austria C-112/00*), and the protection of a national industry (*Cinethique 60* and *61/84*).

4. A second rule from *Cassis*, the rule of mutual recognition, was that if a product was lawfully produced and marketed in one Member State then it should be able to circulate freely throughout the Community (since clarified by the Commission), but this can be rebutted (*Commission v Germany 174/84 (German Beer Purity*)).

5. However, the ECJ has also recognised that Art 34 has been used too often in attempts only to subvert national law which has no effect on imports (*Keck and Mithouard C-267/91 and 268/91 (joined cases)*, where the ECJ held that the *Cassis de Dijon* principle will not apply to selling arrangements that apply to all relevant traders in the Member State, and that apply to both imports and domestic goods in the same way).

6. Selling arrangements also do not breach Art 34 and have included:

   ■ restrictions on opening hours, e.g. Sunday trading (*Punto Casa C-69 and 258/93*);
   ■ sales through specific outlets (*Quietlynn v Southend BC C-23/89*);
   ■ advertising restrictions (*Hunermund 362/88 and Leclerc C-412/93*).

7.5 Art 35 and exports

1. The ECJ takes a different approach to exports and Art 35.
2. Originally, the *Dassonville* formula was assumed to apply.

Flow chart illustrating the means of establishing breach of Art 34

3. But the ECJ has ruled that Art 35 only restricts measures that are designed to differentiate between the domestic and export trade of a Member State so as to confer a benefit on exports at the expense of other states (*Groenveld BV v Produktschap voor Veer en Vlees 15/79*).

4. So, measures applying equally to domestic products for the national market and those for export do not offend Art 35 (*Oebel 155/80*).

5. However, direct discrimination involving distinctly applicable measures does (*Bouhelier 53/76*).

8

Art 30 and customs tariffs, and Art 110 and discriminatory taxation

---

Art 30 and prohibitions on customs duties and measures having equivalent effect:

- Introduced to prevent Member States from subverting the single market by use of customs duties.
- Art 30 is directly effective (*Van Gend en Loos v Nederlandse Administratie des Belastingen*).
- The ECJ provides definition of MHEE – 'any pecuniary charge ... imposed unilaterally on domestic or foreign goods [because] they cross a frontier and which is not a customs duty' (*Commission v Italy and Simmenthal v Italian Minister for Finance*).
- So, a disguised charge may be invalid (*Social Fonds voor de Diamantarbeiders*).

ART 30 AND CUSTOMS DUTIES
ART 110 AND DISCRIMINATORY TAXATION

Art 110 and prohibitions on discriminatory taxation:

- Two aspects to Art 110:
   - (i)   no Member States should impose, directly or indirectly, on products of other Member States internal taxation in excess of that imposed on similar domestic products;
   - (ii) no Member States should impose an internal tax of such a nature to give protection to domestic products.
- To breach Art 110 the tax must discriminate against imports, e.g. applying sliding scales (*Humbold v Directeur des Services Fiscaux*) or only applying tax to imports (*Bobie v HZA Aachen-Nord*).

8.1 Art 30 and prohibition on customs duties and charges having equivalent effect

1. Customs duties are a very old device of protectionism.

2. So they were one of first mechanisms for the Treaty to attack.

3. To prevent Member States subverting the Treaties by introducing measures not called customs duties but with the same effect, the EC Treaty prohibited any such measures.

4. Ex Art 14-Art 15 removed all tariff barriers in transitional period.

5. Art 30 itself is a 'stand still' article prohibiting the introduction of any customs duties or provision having equivalent effect.

6. Art 30 is also directly effective, so as to be enforceable by citizens (*Van Gend en Loos v Nederlandse Administratie des Belastingen 26/62*).

7. Measures having equivalent effect are more problematic and not defined in the Treaty:

   ■ so a definition is given by ECJ case law: 'any pecuniary charge … imposed unilaterally on domestic or foreign goods (because) they cross a frontier and which is not a customs duty in the strict sense constitutes a charge having equivalent effect … even if it is not imposed for the benefit of the state …' (*Commission v Italy 24/68*);

   ■ reiterated in *Simmenthal v Italian Minister for Finance 35/76* and *Bauhuis v Netherlands State 46/76*.

8. So, a disguised charge may be an obstacle to trade and thus have equivalent effect and be invalid (*Social Fonds voor de Diamantarbeiders 2/69* and *3/69*).

9. But a genuine tax will not, if within the requirements of Art 110.

10. A levy on services is permissible if:

    ■ the cost is proportionate to the service received;
    ■ it is in accordance with EU requirements;
    ■ there is no discrimination between domestic and other EU goods (compare *Bauhuis v Netherlands 46/76* with *Commission v Belgium 132/82*).

8.2 Art 110 and discriminatory taxation

1. Internal taxes may distort trade if differently applied:
   - not preventing free movement but as a disincentive;
   - more favourable tax regimes can have the same effect.

2. There are two aspects to Art 110:
   - no Member States should impose, directly or indirectly, on the products of other Member States' internal taxation in excess of that imposed on similar domestic products;
   - no Member States should impose an internal tax of such a nature to give protection to domestic products.

3. But they should be construed as a whole, not separately (*Fazenda Publica v Americo C-345/93*).

4. Direct taxation is generally taken to refer to income tax, etc.:
   - so Art 110 applies to indirect taxes;
   - and means adopted to harmonise taxes include VAT.

5. 'Internal taxation' is interpreted broadly, so might include:
   - charges levied as a percentage of imported products, not general tax (*Llanelli v Meroni 74/76*);
   - but can take account of, for example, higher cost of domestic raw materials (*Luxembourg v Belgium 2/62* and *3/62*);
   - higher manufacturing costs (*Commission v Italy 28/69*).

6. Similar products are not defined in the Treaty but in case law:
   - the ECJ tends to view similarity in terms of way viewed by consumer rather than actual or potential use (*John Walker v Ministeriet for Skatter 243/86*);
   - tax may be discriminatory if products are not so similar in character but do compete (*Commission v UK 170/78*).

7. Taxation must discriminate against imported products to offend Art 110:
   - will do so particularly if sliding scales are applied (*Humblot v Directeur des Services Fiscaux 112/84*);
   - and where imports but not domestic products are subject to fixed scales (*Bobie v HZA Aachen-Nord 127/75*).

9

Art 45 and the free movement of workers

Definition of worker:

- pursuit of effective and genuine activity (*Levin v Staatsecretaris van Justitie*);
- performs service in return for remuneration (*Lawrie-Blum v Land Baden-Wurttemberg*);
- worker who has lost job but is capable of finding other work (*Hoekstra*);
- part-timer needing supplementary benefit (*Kempf v Staatsecretaris voor Justitie*);
- no formal wage but involved in economic activity (*Steymann v Statsecretaris voor Justitie*);
- person looking for work (*R v Immigration Appeal Tribunal, ex parte Antonissen*);
- but not if not for a genuine reason (*Bettray v Staatsecretaris van Justitie*);
- now Directive 2004/38 incorporates these definitions – (Art 7(3)) identifies situations in which worker status will not be lost:
  - temporarily unable to work through sickness or accident;
  - involuntary unemployment after one year's employment in host state and is registered job seeker;
  - involuntary unemployment after fixed term contract of under a year;
  - involuntary unemployment and embarks on vocational course.

FREE MOVEMENT OF WORKERS

Limitations on free movement

- Art 45(3) and Directive 2004/38 Art 27(1) allow derogations for public policy, public security, public health.
- Public policy for genuine threat to society (*R v Bouchereau*).
- But not if not illegal in host state (*Adoui & Cornaille v Belgium*).
- Public policy or security must be exclusively on conduct of individual concerned (*Van Duyn v The Home Office*).
- Public health Directive 2004/38 Art 29(1) lists prescribed diseases, e.g. TB.
- Art 45(4) permits limiting access to public service on nationality.
- Applies only to civil authority or security of state (*Commission v Belgium*).

Rights of entry and residence

- Directive 2004/38 Art 5(1) – can leave home state to seek employment in another state and enter on production of valid identity card or passport, and get residence permit with relevant documents;
- can enter and look for work (*Proceurer de Roi v Royer*);
- for at least 6 months (*R v Immigration Appeal Tribunal ex parte Antonissen*);
- Directive 2004/38 Art 6 gives all EU citizens automatic right of residence in any Member State for three months.

Equal treatment:

Regulation 1612/68 demands equal treatment in all employment matters, including:

- no limiting offers of employment or number of migrant workers (*Commission v France (Re French Merchant Seamen)*);
- linguistic tests are valid (*Groener v Minister of Education*);
- equal conditions for nationals and migrants in pay, conditions, dismissals (*Wurttembergische Milchvertung-Sudmilch AG v Ugliola*);
- dependents have rights to live with worker irrespective of nationality (*Lebon*).

Definition of families:

- Directive 2004/38 Art 2(2) gives right to spouses, dependants under 21, ascendant relatives and registered partners;
- Directive 2004/38 Art 3(2) also gives rights to any actual family dependents and partners of the worker in a durable relationship;
- and cohabitees (*Netherlands State v Anne Florence Reed*) may be a social advantage to the worker.

Right to remain after employment:

- Directive 2004/38 gives right to remain after five years' continuous residence.

9.1 Introduction

1. This was essential to the creation of the internal market.

2. Art 45 requires free movement of workers within the community.

3. The basis for free movement is in Art 18 'any discrimination on grounds of nationality shall be prohibited …'.

4. Found in Arts 45–48 and regulations and directives.

5. Equivalent rights exist in Art 49 and Art 56 for professionals and businesses.

9.2 The character and extent of Art 45

1. Member States are required to prohibit any discrimination between workers of different states based on nationality.

2. And to apply equality to employment, remuneration and all other conditions of employment, e.g. the same for migrant workers as for workers of the host nation.

3. A state can derogate on public security, public health, or public policy grounds, and exclude from public service.

4. The extent of the right is:
   - to take up offers of work already made;
   - to move freely throughout EU to seek employment;
   - to remain in a Member State for employment under the same conditions as a national of the Member State;
   - to remain after employment.

9.3 The definition of 'worker'

1. Art 45 applies to 'workers', but no definition is provided.

2. So, definition has come from numerous Art 267 references but is now also under Directive 2004/38.

3. 'Citizenship' created in TEU is not the same as a 'worker'.

4. The earliest definition held Art 45 applied only to 'the pursuit of effective and genuine activities to the exclusion of activities of such a small scale as to be regarded as purely marginal and ancillary …' (*Levin v Staatsecretaris van Justitie 53/81*).

5. Essential characteristics of a worker are 'performance of services, under the direction of another, in return for remuneration, for a certain period of time …' (*Lawrie-Blum v Land Baden-Wurttemberg 66/85*).

6. The ECJ has interpreted the definition of 'worker' liberally:
   - a worker who has lost his job but is capable of finding other work (*Hoekstra v Bestuur der Badrijfsvereniging voor Detailhandel en Ambachten 75/63*) and *Leclere and Deaconescu C-43/99*;
   - a part-timer needing supplementary benefit for subsistence (*Kempf v Staatssecretaris voor Justitie 139/85*);
   - a person with no formal wage but involved in an economic activity (*Steymann v Statsecretaris voor Justitie 196/87*) *Trojani C-456/02*;
   - a professional sportsman (*Dona v Mantero 13/76*);
   - a person looking for work (*R v Immigration Appeal Tribunal, ex parte Antonissen 292/89*).

7. However, the ECJ has also imposed limitations:
   - where there is no economic purpose to the activity (*Bettray v Staatsecretaris van Justitie 344/87*);
   - if the sport is not a genuine economic activity (*Walrave & Koch v Association Union Cycliste Internationale 36/74*).

8. Directive 2004/38 also identifies situations where worker status is not lost:
   - a worker temporarily unable to work through sickness or accident;
   - involuntary unemployment after one year employment in the host state and the worker is a registered job seeker;
   - involuntary unemployment after a fixed term contract of under a year;
   - involuntary unemployment and the worker takes a vocational course.

9.4 Workers' families

1. Art 45 gives rights to workers' families:
   - Directive 2004/38 provides a new definition of family members in Art 2(2): a) a spouse; b) a registered partner (where the host state treats registered partners as equivalent to marriage); c) direct descendants under 21 who are dependants, and those of the partner; d) dependent direct ascending relatives;
   - Art 3(2) also includes a) any other family members whether EU citizens or not who are dependents or require personal care of

worker; b) a partner with whom the EU citizen has a durable relationship, i.e. genuine cohabitees.

2. Sometimes rights extend to cohabitees (*Netherlands State v Anne Florence Reed 59/85*) if ensures equal social and tax advantages to worker.

3. Rights are not lost through mere separation (*Diatta v Land Berlin 267/83*).

4. But may be with complete marital breakdown (*R v Secretary of State for the Home Department, ex parte Sandhu* (1985)).

9.5 Rights of entry and residence

1. These rights are identified in Directive 2004/38 Art 5(1):
   - to leave home state to seek employment in another state;
   - to enter another state 'on production of a valid identity card or passport (or proof of relationship with the worker) …' (non-EU nationals need visas);
   - to notify the relevant authorities.

2. By Directive 2004/38 Art 6 all EU citizens have right of residence in any other Member State for up to three months on production of a passport or identity card – non-EU family members accompanying the EU national have the same rights but require a visa. Under Directive 2004/38 Art 16(1) permanent right of residence is gained after five years continuous residence.

3. The right includes to enter and look for work (*Proceurer de Roi v Royer 48/75*).

4. There is no fixed time-limit, but six months has been held sufficient, justifying removal if past (*R v Immigration Appeal Tribunal, ex parte Antonissen C-292/89*) (three months in *Royer*). Under Directive 2004/38 the worker is allowed to stay until he becomes an unreasonable burden on the state.

5. Failures to observe formalities do not justify refusal to allow entry or residence (*R v Pieck 157/79*).

6. Nor do they justify deportation (*Watson & Bellman 118/75*).

7. Seasonal workers are allowed temporary residence permits.

9.6 The right to equal treatment

1. Art 45 requires abolition of discrimination on nationality in employment, remuneration and conditions.

2. Regulation 1612/68 requires equal treatment in all employment matters and elimination of obstacles to mobility. It has three Titles:
   - Title I – eligibility for employment:
     - (i) Art 3 prohibits limiting offers of employment or restricting numbers of migrant workers (*Commission v France (Re French Merchant Seamen) 167/73*);
     - (ii) Art 5 no discriminatory tests for recruitment, e.g. vocational, medical or other;
     - (iii) linguistic tests are valid (*Groener v Minister of Education 378/87*).
   - Title II – equality in conditions of employment:
     - (i) Art 7(1) ensures equal conditions for nationals and migrants in pay, conditions, dismissals, etc. (*Wurttembergische Milchvertung-Sudmilch AG v Ugliola 15/69; Sotgiu v Deutsche Bundepost 152/73* and *Kobler C-224/0* and *Merida C-400/02*);
     - (ii) by Art 7(2) migrants should receive the same tax and social advantages as nationals which may survive the death of the worker (*Fiorini v SNCF 32/75*);
     - (iii) the right exists whether or not linked to a contract of employment (*Ministere Public v Even 207/78*);
     - (iv) social advantage can include, for example, a grant (*Brown 197/86*);
     - (v) access to social advantages is conditional on worker status – so to gain social security benefits, a work-seeker must be genuinely seeking work but a denial of those benefits must be objective and proportionate (*Collins C-138/02* and *Ioannidis C-258/04*).
   - Title III – workers' families.
     - (i) Art 10(1) gave family, if dependants, rights to live with worker irrespective of their nationality (*Lebon 316/85*); now Directive 2004/38 Art 14(1) guarantees the right but;
     - (ii) Art 11 gives the right to take employment regardless of nationality (*Gul 131/85*);
     - (iii) Art 12 gives workers' children the same rights as nationals to education, training and apprenticeship:
       - a) so they can receive grants (*GBC Echtemach and A Moritz v Netherlands Minister for Education 389/87 and 390/87*);

b) and may be exempt from fees if nationals are (*Forcheri v Belgian State 152/82*);

c) ECJ takes a broad view of 'vocational training' which may include university degrees (*Gravier v Liege 293/83* and *Blaizot v University of Liege 24/86*);

d) and Art 12 rights continue even on death of worker (*Michel 76/62* and *Casagrande 9/74*).

9.7 The right permanent residence under Directive 2004/38

1. By Art 16(1) all EU citizens gain the right to permanent residence after a period of five years continuous residence in the host state.

2. The same rule applies to non-EU family members who have lived in the host state continuously for five years with the citizen.

3. Under Art 16(3) continuous residence is not affected by:
   (i) temporary absences under six months in a year;
   (ii) absences for military service;
   (iii) one absence for up to 12 months for e.g. pregnancy, illness, vocational training etc.

4. Under Art 17 permanent residence can also be gained under the five-year qualifying period if the EU citizen who is a worker or self-employed;
   (i) has reached retirement age;
   (ii) becomes permanently incapable of working;
   (iii) lives in the host state but works in another state.

5. Also under Art 17 families of the EU citizen who is a worker or self-employed also gain permanent residence if the worker dies before the five years, provided that
   (i) the worker/self employed person had resided for two continuous years in the host state;
   (ii) the death occurred because of accident at work or occupational disease;
   (iii) the surviving spouse lost nationality of the state following marriage.

9.8 Free movement and professional sport

1. Sport, particularly football, raises problems under Art 45, i.e. transfer system, limitations on numbers of foreign players.

2. The ability of managers to move freely throughout the community has been established (*UNECTEF v Heylens 222/86*).

3. The ECJ in the *Bosman* ruling has major implications for football:
   ■ Art 45 prohibits transfer fees once a contract has terminated;
   ■ it restricts numbers (*Bosman C-415/93*).

9.9 Social security provisions

1. Art 48 requires aggregation of all periods of work in the community for eligibility to benefits.

2. Implemented by Regulation 1408/71 – did not harmonise social security systems but required application of systems so as not to penalise worker and prevent him using Art 45.

3. The key principles were:
   ■ universality of eligibility and of benefits;
   ■ non-discrimination (meaning migrant workers cannot be excluded from national systems);
   ■ aggregated and not concurrent benefits.

4. In 2010 Regulation 883/2004 (as amended by Regulation 988/2009) replaced Regulation 1408/71:
   ■ its scope is broader than the earlier Regulation as it applies not just to the employed/self-employed and their families, but others who are not economically active;
   ■ it simplifies the procedure and aims to facilitate free movement of citizens irrespective of economic status.

9.10 Limitations on free movement

1. Contained in Art 45(3) – Member States can introduce rules which limit the exercise of free movement based 'on grounds of public policy, public security or public health …'.

2. Directive 2004/38 Art 27(1) lays down principles on all three – extends to all Community nationals who reside in or travel in another Member State, as employees, self-employed, or as families.

3. Art 27(1) – derogation cannot be used for economic ends.

4. By Art 27(2), measures taken on public policy or public security:
   - must be taken exclusively on the conduct of the individual concerned (*Van Duyn v The Home Office 41/74*);
   - and personal conduct is strictly interpreted (*Rutili v Ministère de l'Interieure 36/75*);
   - and must comply with the principle of proportionality (*Watson and Bellman 118/75*);
   - and a restriction on movement is permissible only if it is objectively justified (*Omega C-36/02*).

5. Public policy can only be invoked where there is a genuine present and sufficiently serious threat to the interests of society (*R v Bouchereau 30/77*). Also:
   - past convictions alone are insufficient to invoke the exception Art 27(2) (*Bonsignore v Oberstadtdirecktor of the City of Cologne 67/74* and *Oliveri C-493/01*);
   - exclusion cannot be for activity not illegal in the host state (*Adoui and Cornaille v Belgian State 115/81 and 116/81*);
   - mere expiry of an ID card or passport is never sufficient ground for deportation (*Watson and Bellman 118/75*).

6. The difference between public policy and public security is vague.

7. Art 29 identifies prescribed diseases justifying refusal of entry:
   - those with epidemic potential as defined by the relevant instruments of the World Health Organization;
   - other infectious diseases or other contagious parasitic diseases if they are subject to protection provisions applying to nationals of the host state.

8. Procedural safeguards include:
   - by Art 30(1) the decision to exclude/deport must be notified in writing in a manner that the recipient can understand;
   - by Art 30(2) the grounds for the decision must be given in full;
   - by Art 30(3) they must be notified of the appeals procedure;
   - by Art 31 they have access to judicial and appropriate administrative redress which must determine that the decision is not disproportionate.

9.11 Public service employment

1. Art 45(4) allows Member States to deny/restrict access to workers in public service on the basis of their nationality.

2. But the ECJ has interpreted this provision fairly narrowly:
   - it does not apply to all public service, only exercise of civil authority or security of state (*Commission v Belgium (Re Public Employees) 149/79*);
   - it applies only to access to employment, not to conditions (*Sotgiu v Deutsche Bundespost 152/73*);
   - so cannot reserve posts in hospitals for nationals (*Commission v France (Re French Nurses) 307/84*);
   - or in teaching (*Bleis v Ministere de l'Education C-4/91*);
   - or impose unnecessary qualifications on non-nationals (*Groener Minister for Education 397/87*).

10

Art 49 and freedom of establishment Art 56 and the right to provide services

---

Art 49 and freedom of establishment

- Grants individuals the right to establish a profession or business in another Member State, or to set up an agency, branch or subsidiary.
- Art 49 is directly applicable, so no need to introduce directives (*Reyners v The Belgian State*).
- It is also directly effective and has been applied, e.g. to lawyers (*Thieffrey v Conseil a l'Ordre des Avocates a la court de Paris*).
- The main obstacle is national qualifications.
- Three methods used to resolve this problem:
    (i)   harmonisation through individual directives;
    (ii) ECJ developed principle of equivalence of qualifications;
    (iii) mutual recognition originally under Directive 89/48. Now these are incorporated in Directive 2005/36, the Recognition of Professional Qualifications Directive.

RIGHTS OF ESTABLISHMENT AND PROVISION OF SERVICES

Freedom to provide services:

- Art 56 appropriate for those wishing to provide services without settling in the host nation.
- By Art 57 these are services of an industrial and commercial character, craftsmanship and the exercise of a profession.
- Right is directly effective, so claimants subject to same rules as national (*Van Binsbergen v Bestuur van de Bedrijfsvereniging voor de Metaainijverheid*).
- Right is also to receive as well as to provide services (*Luisi and Carbone v Ministero del Tesoro*).
- But right requires an economic element (*SPUC v Grogan*).

10.1 Introduction

1. Both rights were essential to the creation of a single market.

2. The right to establish is contained in Arts 49–54:
   - It refers to the right of free movement of both the self-employed and professionals.
   - It can include 'legal' as well as natural persons.
   - It is the right to set up and carry out a business, trade or profession in another Member State.

3. The freedom to provide services is in Arts 56–62. It complements the right of establishment by allowing a person established in one state to exercise a business or profession in another state, not linked to residence.

4. The difference between establishment and providing services was identified in *Gebhard C-55/94* – establishment is where the person participates 'on a stable and continuous basis' whereas providing a service is pursuing an activity 'on a temporary basis'.

5. There is an obvious overlap between the two principles, and some similarity with Art 45 – and both are subject to the same derogations in Directive 2004/38, which also provides rights of entry and residence.

6. In either case the requirement is that the person should be subject to the same condition as nationals.

7. The major barrier to the freedoms is national qualifications or requirements.

10.2 Freedom of establishment

1. Art 49 provides that 'restrictions on the freedom of establishment of nationals of one member state in the territory of another shall be prohibited … such prohibition shall also apply to restrictions on the setting up of agencies, branches or subsidiaries …'.

2. Art 49 is directly applicable, so introducing Directives is not vital (*Reyners v The Belgian State 2/74*). Although harmonising directives was the means anticipated for dealing with the problem of different qualifications in different Member States.

3. It is also directly effective, so can be applied in a variety of circumstances:

- *Thieffrey v Conseil a l'Ordre des Avocates a la cour de Paris 71/76* and lawyers;
- *Patrick v Ministre des Affaires Culturelles 11/77* and architects;
- *Van Ameyde v Ufficio Centrale Italiano di Assistenza Assiscurativa Automobilisti in Circolazione Internazionale 90/76* and a motor insurance claims investigator.

4. The main barrier to the freedoms is national regulation of trades and professions based on national qualifications.

5. Three methods were devised to resolve this problem:
   - harmonisation of professional qualifications through 'sectoral' Directives;
   - 'mutual recognition' of qualifications by Directive 89/48, Directive 92/51 and the 'Slim' Directive 2001/19;
   - 'equivalence' of qualifications using the principle of non-discrimination; now these have been incorporated in Directive 2005/36, the Recognition of Professional Qualifications Directive.

6. Harmonisation was achieved only by a complex, time consuming process of introducing individual directives for individual trades, e.g.:
   - retail trade and Directive 68/363;
   - doctors and Directive 93/16;
   - architects and Directive 85/384;
   - lawyers and Directive 77/249 (but only limited rights to practice).

   The effect was that a person qualified in one state could then automatically practise in another.

7. Mutual recognition was developed because harmonisation was too time consuming and impossible in certain areas. Directive 89/48 introduced a general system for mutual recognition of 'higher education diplomas':
   - These are qualifications taking three years or more.
   - The directive applies if no harmonising directive exists.
   - This means that Member States must assess the equivalence of qualifications of other states so that a person can establish without needing to re-qualify.
   - However, a substantial difference can lead to requirement of an aptitude test or an adaptation period.
   - This was supplemented by Directive 92/51 in respect of one-year year vocational qualifications.
   - And since then by the Slim Directive 2001/19 requiring Member States to take into account work experience and qualifications gained in third countries.

8. Where there is no harmonising directive and mutual recognition cannot apply the principle of non-discrimination can be used *Steinhauser v City of Biarritz 197/84* and the established principles in, e.g., *Reyners, Thieffrey, Patrick:*
   - the Member State must asses the equivalency of the person's qualifications (*UNECTEF v Heylens 222/86*)
   - and must give reasons why not and allow appeal (*Vlassopoulou C-340/89*).

9. Directive 2005/36 has incorporated the sectoral directives and introduced a new simpler and fairer process of mutual recognition of qualifications. In respect of the principle of non-discrimination formerly developed in the case law, where either sectoral directives or mutual recognition do not apply, there is a requirement of non-discrimination and proportionality.
   - Arts 10–15 provide for a general system of recognition of professional qualifications – so acts as a fall-back for qualifications falling outside of the previous processes – obviously adaptation tests/periods still apply;
   - Arts 16–20 provide an automatic system of recognition based on prior professional experience in certain defined areas;
   - Arts 21–49 provide a system of automatic recognition of qualification in specific professions, e.g. doctors, nurses, dentists, vets, midwives, pharmacists and architects.

10.3 The freedom to provide and receive services

1. Art 56 provides for the abolition of restrictions on the freedom to provide services by non-nationals who are not established in the state of the recipient. So is designed for those wishing to provide services without settling in the host nation.

2. Services are identified in Art 57 as those normally provided for remuneration, not related to free movement of capital, goods or workers, 'of an industrial and commercial character, craftsmanship and the exercise of a profession ...'.

3. The right is directly effective:
   - so claimants are subject to the same rules of professional conduct as nationals (*Van Binsbergen v Bestuur van de Bedrijfsvereniging voor de Metaalnijverheid 33/74*);
   - but the right can only be denied where there is an imperative reason of public interest (*Omega C-36/02*).

4. The important corollary of the rule is the enforceable freedom to receive services (*Luisi and Carbone v Ministero del Tesoro 286/82*):
   - this principle has been extended to cover access to education and vocational training (*Gravier v City of Liege 293/83*);
   - so vocational courses must be offered on equal terms to all EU citizens (*Blaizot v University of Liege 24/86*);
   - but state, secondary education is not a service (*Belgium v Humbel 263/86*);
   - and maintenance grants are outside of the scope of the article (*Brown v Secretary of State for Scotland 197/86*).

5. The principle of non-discrimination has been extended out further to include receipt of state compensation (*Cowan v French Treasury 186/87*).

6. However, this is unavailable without an economic element (*SPUC v Grogan C-159/80*).

11

EU competition law

11.1 The purpose and character of competition law

11.1.1 The purpose of competition law

1. Art 2 EC Treaty (now Art 4 TEU) sees the task of EU law as 'the promotion of harmonious development of economic activities by the creation of a common market and the progressive approximation of the economic policies of the Member States...'.

2. The EU is also bound to ensure that 'competition in the internal market is not distorted...'.

3. So, the framers of the original Treaty:
   - recognised that unfettered market forces can lead directly to anti-competitive practices;
   - inserted rules to deal with this based on the Sherman Act model.

4. These rules had three principal objectives:
   - to avoid restrictive practices and agreements (Art 101);
   - to prevent large businesses from abusing their market dominance (Art 102);
   - to apply similar rules to the public sector (Art 106).

5. EU competition law is criticised because:
   - all practices are treated alike, even if they would benefit the consumer;
   - policy has been said to sacrifice equity and efficiency to political goals;
   - Ian Ward says its existence is 'a perversity' and 'the loud admission of defeat' and 'an admission that the market alone cannot effect competition';
   - there is always the danger of Member States clinging to national interests.

6. But the EU has succeeded in framing cohesive and consistent objectives, identified in the Commission's Ninth Report on Competition Policy:
   - creation of an open and unified market not partitioned by restrictive and anti-competitive agreements;
   - realisation of effective competition avoiding over-concentration or abuses by dominant companies;
   - achieving fairness in the market place, giving support to small and medium sized firms, protecting the consumer, and penalising unlawful state subsidies;
   - maintaining the competitive position of the EU against rivals in global economy.

11.1.2 The character of competition law

1. It covers everything – goods, services and intellectual property rights.

2. Provisions are framed in broad terms, so are subject to ECJ interpretation.

3. It can be used against firms regardless of existence of registered office in the EU.

4. Rules are pragmatic, so are subject to exceptions to preserve market efficiency.

5. Penalties apply where trade in the EU is affected, so can apply to small firms and inter-state disputes

6. So, it is possible for EU law and national law to co-exist (*Wilhelm v Bundeskartellamt 23/67*).

7. Art 101 and Art 102 are complementary, pursuing the same objectives by focusing on different types of activity.

The basic Art 101 prohibition:

- Rule prohibits 'agreements between undertakings, decisions of associations of undertakings and concerted practices which may affect trade between Member States having as object prevetion, restriction or distortion of competition within internal market'.
- Undertakings defined by ECJ as 'single organisation of personal, tangible and intangible elements, attached to an autonomous legal entity and pursuing a long term economic aim' (*Mannesmann v High Authority*), e.g. a trade association (*FRUGO v Commission*).
- Commission can grant exemption.

ART 101 AND RESTRICTIVE PRACTICES

Activities beyond scope of Art 101:

Commission Notice on agreement of minor importance:
- if less than 10% market share for horizontal agreements; 15% for vertical agreements;
- commercial agents and subsidiaries.

Exemptions if:
- contributes to improving production or distribution of goods or promoting technical or economic progress (*Transocean Marine Paint Association*);
- consumer gets fair share of benefit (*ACEC v Berliet*);
- no unnecessary restrictions (*Consten and Grundig v Commission*);
- no risk of eliminating competition (*Re Fine Papers*);
- can be individual or block.

Elements proving breach of Art 101:

Agreements between undertakings, decisions by associations of undertakings, concerted practices:
- must involve collusive behaviour (*AEG Telefunken v Commission*);
- decisions by associations of undertakings are usually by trade associations on, e.g. fixing discounts, collective boycotts, restrictive contract clauses;
- concerted practices are a form of co-ordination between enterprises that has not yet reached the point where it is a contract (*ICI Ltd v Commission (The Dyestuffs Case)*);
- Art 101 identifies some prohibited arrangements, e.g.:

  (i) price fixing (*VBVB and VVVB v Comission*);

  (ii) limiting production (*The Quinine Cartel* case);

  (iii) sharing markets or suppliers (*Siemens/Franc*);

  (iv) applying dissimilar conditions to equivalent transactions (*IZA International Belgium*).

Affecting trade between Member States:
- ascertained by reference to free movement and attainment of single market;
- must be capable of constituting a threat, direct or indirect, actual or potential, on the pattern of trade (*Belasco v Commission*);
- no need to prove harm, just that agreement may prevent, restrict or distort competition sufficiently (*Vereniging van Cementhandelaren v Commission*).

Object or effect of preventing, restricting or distorting competition:
- as much to do with practical outcomes as intentions;
- key issue is whether or not competition is affected (*Consten and Grundig v Commission*);
- ECJ try to apply the rules so as not to stifle enterprise and initiative (*Société Technique Miniere v Maschinenbau Ulm*).

11.2 Art 101 and restrictive practices

11.2.1 The basic prohibition in Art 101

1. By Art 101, 'All agreements between undertakings, decisions of associations of undertakings and concerted practices which may affect trade between Member States and which have as their object or effect the prevention, restriction or distortion of competition within the internal market' are prohibited.

2. Art 101 also gives particular examples of anti-competitive acts – those which:

   ■ directly or indirectly fix purchase or selling prices or any other trading conditions;
   ■ limit or control production, markets, technical development or investment;
   ■ share markets or sources of supply;
   ■ apply dissimilar conditions to equivalent transactions with other trading parties, thereby placing them at a competitive disadvantage;
   ■ make the conclusion of contracts subject to acceptance by the other parties of supplementary obligations which, by their nature, have no connection with the subject of such contracts.

3. Art 101(2) makes all such agreements void. The Commission formerly granted exemptions and negative clearance; now the process of applying exemptions is internally dealt with within the Member State.

4. Both Art 101 and Art 102 concern conduct of 'undertakings'.

   ■ The term is not defined in the Treaty, but is given a broad definition by the ECJ: 'a single organisation of personal, tangible and intangible elements, attached to an autonomous legal entity and pursuing a long term economic aim…' (*Mannesmann v High Authority* (1962)).
   ■ It can therefore cover everything from an individual to a multi-national corporation.
   ■ It has included, for example:
      (i)   an opera singer (*Re Unitel 78/516*);
      (ii) a sports federation (*Re World Cup 1990 Package Tours 92/521*);
      (iii) a state-owned corporation (*Italian State v Sacchi 155/73*);
      (iv) a public agency (*Hofner v Macroton C-41/90*);
      (v)   a trade association (*FRUGO v Commission 71/74*);
   ■ but must involve some form of economic activity (*FENIN v Commission T-319/99*) but the Court of Justice has taken a

different view in relation to the International Olympic Committee (*Meca-Medina and Macjen v Commission C-519/04P*).

11.2.2 The elements of proof for an action under Art 101

Agreements between undertakings, decisions by associations of undertakings, concerted practices

1. Agreements: always involve some sort of collusive behaviour as distinct from unilateral acts (*AEG Telefunken v Commission 107/82*):
   - can include informal, oral agreements (*Tepea 28/77*);
   - and the so-called 'gentlemen's agreements' (*ACF Chemiefarma v Commission 41,44,45/69 (The Quinine Cartel Case)*).
   - but must involve autonomous behaviour – so not an agreement imposed by national law (*Commission and France v Ladbroke Racing Ltd C359 and 379/95P*);

2. Decisions by associations:
   - usually involve rules of trade associations;
   - and prohibited decisions would include: recommending prices, fixing discounts, collective boycotts, restrictive contract clauses;
   - and even non-binding recommendations (*Vereniging van Cementhandelaren v Commission 8/72*).

3. Concerted practices have been defined by the ECJ as: 'a form of co-ordination between enterprises that has not yet reached the point where it is a contract in the true sense of the word, but which, in practice, consciously substitutes co-operation for the risks of competition …' (*ICI Ltd v Commission 48/69 (The Dyestuffs Case)*).
   - The Court of Justice has held that even a single meeting by undertakings can amount to a concerted practice (*T-Mobile Netherlands BV and Others v Raad van bestuur van der Nederlandse Mededingsautoriteit C-47/09*).

4. The test is where parallel behaviour is co-operative, so lacks independence (*Co-operatieve Vereeniging 'Suiker Unie' v Commission 40-48,50,54-56,111,113,114/73 (The Sugar Cartel Case)*).

5. Agreements may be:
   - horizontal, i.e. between competitors, and may, for example, divide up markets (*The Dyestuffs Case*); or

- vertical, i.e. between undertakings at different levels in the process, and may be, for example, exclusive distribution arrangements, or licensing agreements.

6. The article identifies specific prohibited arrangements:

- Price fixing, which may be agreements on, for example, discounts, credit, etc., and have included:
    (i) agreements between zinc producers (*Re Zinc Producers Group*);
    (ii) agreements between Italian glass manufacturers (*Re Italian Flat Glass Cartel*);
    (iii) a retail price maintenance agreement between Belgian and Dutch booksellers (*VBVB and VVVB v Commission 43 and 63/82*).

- Limiting production, where undertakings restrict their own growth to artificially raise prices and prevent outsiders entering the agreement (*The Quinine Cartel case*).

- Sharing markets or sources of supply:
    (i) can involve carving up markets (either geographically or by product);
    (ii) and is common in oligopolies where competitors give each other exclusive dealerships (*Siemens/Franc 1985*).

- Applying dissimilar conditions to equivalent transactions:
    (i) to place another party at a disadvantage;
    (ii) so might involve giving advantageous conditions to another party (*IZA International Belgium 96–102, 104, 105, 108, 110/82*).

- Imposing supplementary obligations: those with no relationship with actual subject of contract.

Affecting trade between Member States

1. In order to breach Art 101 the agreement must affect trade between Member States.

2. This is ascertained by reference to the free movement of goods and attainment of a single market.

3. So it must be capable of constituting a threat 'direct or indirect, actual or potential, on the pattern of trade…' (*Belasco v Commission 246/86*).

4. So there is no need to prove actual harm as long as the agreement is likely to prevent, restrict or distort competition to a sufficient degree (*Vereniging van Cementhandelaren v Commission 8/72*).

The object or effect of preventing, restricting or distorting competition

1. 'Object' and 'effect' are clearly meant to be alternatives, so the test is as much to do with practical outcomes as intentions

2. So, the key issue is whether competition has been affected, not whether trade has gone up or down (*Consten and Grundig v Commission 56 and 58/64*).

3. The ECJ tries to apply the rules so as not to stifle enterprise and initiative (*Société Technique Miniere v Maschinenbau Ulm 56/65*).

4. It will also apply the *de minimis* rule (*Frans Volk v Establissments Vervaecke Sprl 5/69*).

11.2.3 Activities falling outside of the scope of Art 101

1. Undertakings used to be able to obtain negative clearance or comfort letters from the Commission but now competition law is administered by national authorities

2. Commission Notice on Minor Agreements 2001 – agreements not caught by Art 101 if less than a 10% market share for the goods or services in the area of the common market covered by the agreement if horizontal, or 15% if vertical – though a blacklist exists of agreements not tolerated whatever the level of effect.

3. Commercial relations to which the rules do not apply:
   - commercial agents, where they are simply concerned with negotiating transactions for the principal, and assume no financial risk;
   - subsidiaries and parent companies, as the subsidiary has no autonomous decision making capacity (but may breach Art 102).

4. Exemptions:
   - Art 101(3) creates criteria for exempting agreements.
   - There are four conditions (two positive, two negative) to be met before exemption is granted:
      (i) the agreement, decision or practice must contribute to improving production or distribution of goods or promoting technical or economic progress (*Transocean Marine Paint Association (D1967) and Re Vacuum Interrupters (No 1) (D1977)*);

(ii) a fair share of the resulting benefit must accrue to the consumer, which is not merely the end consumer (*ACEC v Berliet* (D1968));

(iii) no unnecessary restrictions should be imposed, e.g. absolute territorial protections (*Consten and Grundig v Commission*);

(iv) there must be no possibility of the restrictions eliminating competition in respect of a substantial part of the product in question (*Re Fine Papers* (D1972)).

■ Individual exemptions.

Used to be granted under Regulation 17/62 by notice to Commission. Now under Regulation 1/2003 process is operated by Member States.

■ Block exemptions:

(i) introduced to reduce the bureaucratic burden of applications for individual exemptions;

(ii) granted in Regulations covering specific types of agreements;

(iii) Examples include:

- exclusive distribution: 1983/83;
- exclusive purchasing: 1984/83;
- patent licensing: 2349/84;
- motor vehicle distribution: 123/85;
- know-how licensing: 556/89;
- Regulation 2790/99 exempts all vertical agreements except certain serious restraints;
- research and development agreements: 2658/2000.

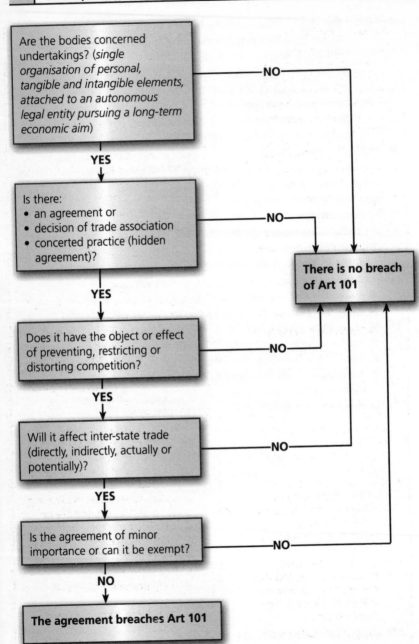

How a breach of Art 101 is established

The basic prohibition:

- Art 102 involves the concentration of economic power in an undertaking.
- Any abuse of commercial dominance is prohibited if it would affect trade between Member States.
- Art 102 can also apply to oligopolies (*The Flat Glass* case).
- Exemptions are not available (except for mergers).
- Three requirements:
  (i) dominant position in market;
  (ii) abuse of dominant position;
  (iii) affects trade between Member States.

AN ART 102 ABUSE OF A DOMINANT POSITION

The abuse:

- Defined in case law as behaviour which influences structure of market so that competition is weakened, and maintenance or growth of competition is hindered.
- So could include, e.g.
  - differential pricing for different Member States (*United Brands*);
  - 'tying arrangements' (*Tetra Pak II*);
  - dissimilar conditions;
  - limiting markets, technical development, production (*Magill TV Guide & ITP v Commission*).

Affecting inter-state trade:

- must result from the abuse.

Existence of dominance:

- Dominance defined in ECSC Treaty – undertaking holds position shielding it against effective competition.
- The ECJ has also defined dominance and 'the power to control production or distribution for a significant part of the products in question' (*Continental Can Co. v Commission*) and 'a position of economic strength … which enables it to prevent competition being maintained' (*United Brands*).
- Need to consider:
  (i) relevant market;
  (ii) market share.
- Relevant product market decided on whether there is sufficient interchangeability between all the products forming part of the same market (*Hoffman-la-Roche v Commission*).
- So could be, e.g. separate cartons for pasteurised and UHT milk (*Tetra Pak (No 1)*).
- Geographical market should be whole EU, but can take into account other factors, e.g. costs and feasibility of transport (*Hilti v Commission*).
- Temporal market may involve, e.g. seasonal factors (*United Brands*).
- No particular market share needed for dominance, e.g. 40% share in United Brands insufficient.
- Should consider, e.g.:
  (i) market share *Hoffman-la-Roche*);
  (ii) competitor's share (*United Brands*).

11.3 Art 102 and abuse of a dominant position

11.3.1 Introduction

1. Art 101 concerns collusion between undertakings, but Art 102 usually concerns actions of a single undertaking.

2. So, the threat to competition is the concentration of economic power.

3. By Art 102, 'Any abuse by one or more undertakings of a dominant position within the internal market or in a substantial part of it shall be prohibited as incompatible with the internal market insofar as it may affect trade between Member States':
   - specific examples of abuses are identified;
   - Art 101 and Art 102 are not mutually exclusive, so there is discretion which to claim under;
   - Art 102 can apply also to oligopolies (*The Flat Glass Case* (D1989)).

4. Art 102 also deals with mergers and concentrations.

5. There are overlaps with Art 101 – exemptions are not available (though they are for mergers).

6. Art 102 does not prohibit dominant positions, only abuses, so is not meant to punish efficient economic behaviour.

7. There are three requirements that must be shown:
   - that the undertaking has a dominant position in the market;
   - that the practice in question abuses that dominant position;
   - that trade between Member States is affected as a result.

11.3.2 The existence of a dominant position

1. Dominance is not defined in the Treaty, but it is in the ECSC Treaty where undertakings hold a position 'shielding them against effective competition in a substantial part of the common market ...'.

2. So it is left to the ECJ, as usual, to define in the cases:
   - 'power to behave independently without taking into account their competitors, purchasers or suppliers because of their share of the market or ... availability of technical knowledge, raw materials or capital, they have power to control production or distribution for significant part of products' (*Continental Can Co. v Commission 6/72*);

- 'a position of economic strength ... which enables it to prevent competition being maintained on the relevant market by giving it the power to behave to an appreciable effect independently of its competitors, and ultimately its consumers' (*United Brands v Commission* 27/76);
- 'such a position does not preclude some competition but enables (it) ... if not to determine, at least to have an appreciable effect on the conditions in which that competition will develop, and in any case to act largely in disregard of it' (*Hoffmann-la-Roche v Commission* 85/76).

3. So there are two key concepts in determining dominance:
   - relevant product market and geographical market;
   - calculation of market share.

The relevant product market

1. Dominant undertakings will want the product market defined broadly; those affected for it to be defined narrowly.

2. So, product market includes the product plus all products which may be perfectly substituted for it.
   - It is measured on whether there is 'sufficient interchangeability between all products forming part of same market insofar as specific use of products is concerned ...' (*Hoffmann-la-Roche v Commission*).
   - The relevant market depends on 'cross elasticity of demand' and 'supply'.

3. Examples of the relevant market have included:
   - heavy goods vehicle tyres as opposed to tyres generally (*Michelin (NV Nederlandsche Baden-Industrie Michelin) v Commission* 322/81);
   - cash register parts (*Hugin Kassaregister AB v Commission* 22/78);
   - separate cartons for pasteurised and UHT milk (*Tetra Pak (No 1)* T-51/89).

Geographical market

1. This is 'where the conditions of competition are sufficiently homogenous for the effect of economic power on the undertaking to be evaluated ...' (*United Brands*).

2. In general, the relevant market must be the whole EU, but situations of producers in busy commercial areas are different to those in remote rural areas, even if they enjoy the same market share.

3. So other things will inevitably be taken into account:
   ■ cost, feasibility of transport (*Hilti v Commission T-30/89*);
   ■ pattern/volume of consumption (*Suiker Unie 40/73*).

Temporal market

1. Seasonal factors may be relevant if there is no substitution (*United Brands*).

Calculation of market share

1. No particular market share is required to prove dominance, e.g. a 40% share in *United Brands* was not sufficient on its own – other factors were relevant, e.g. owned own fleet, could control volume of other imports, and highly fragmented rest of market.

2. So other factors must be considered, e.g.:
   ■ competitors' market share was 10% and 16% in *United Brands*;
   ■ superior technological knowledge and sales network in *Michelin*;
   ■ control of production/distribution in *Hoffmann-la-Roche*;
   ■ conduct/performance.

11.3.3 The abuse of the dominant position

1. The abuse, not existence, of dominant position is prohibited.

2. There is no definition of abuse in the article – though there are some examples.

3. So, again it is defined by the ECJ: 'behaviour ... which is such as to influence the structure of the market where, as a result of the very presence of the undertaking in question, the degree of competition is weakened, and ... has the effect of hindering the maintenance of the degree of competition ... or the growth of that competition ...'.

4. Specific practices identified as abuses in the Article include:

- directly or indirectly imposing unfair purchase or selling prices or other unfair trading conditions, e.g.:
  - (i)   price reduction to kill competition (*AKZO v Commission C-62/86*);
  - (ii) differential pricing for different states (*United Brands*);
  - (iii) loyalty rebates (*Hoffmann-la-Roche*);
- limiting production, markets or technical development to the prejudice of consumers (*Magill TV Guide and ITP v Commission C-241/91 P*); can include exclusive supply agreements (*Hoffman La Roche*) or a refusal to supply (*Sot. Lelos kai Sia EE and Others v GlaxoSmithKline AECE Farmakeftikon Proionton C-468/06 to 478/06*);
- applying dissimilar conditions to equivalent transactions with other trading parties, thereby placing them at a competitive disadvantage;
- making conclusion of contracts subject to supplementary obligations having no connection with subject of such contracts, e.g. 'tying arrangements' (*Tetra Pak II (1992)*).

11.3.4 Affecting trade between Member States

1. This must be an effect caused by the abuse.

2. The same condition is imposed in Art 101.

3. It is not hard to show.

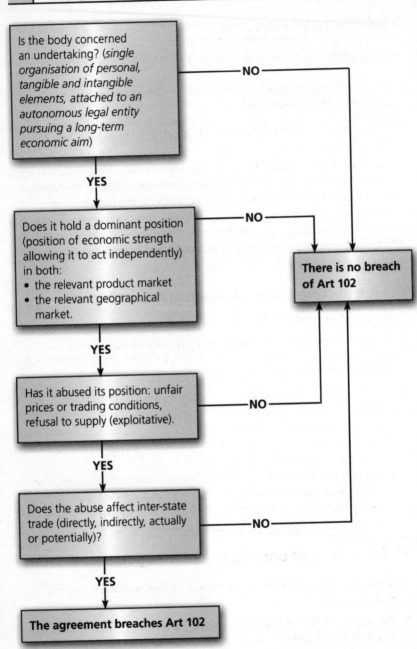

The means of esablishing a breach of Art 102

11.4 Merger control

11.4.1 Merger control under Art 101 and Art 102

1. Prior to 1990 only standard competition law was available to deal with mergers and concentrations.

2. Both needed control because the nature of monopoly power is anti-competitive.

3. So, Art 102 might be infringed if a dominant undertaking strengthened its dominance so that the only undertakings to remain in the relevant market are those whose behaviour depends on the dominant one (*Europemballage Corporation and Continental Can v Commission 6/72*).

11.4.2 Merger control originally under Regulation 4064/89

1. Pressure for effective legislation grew by late 1980s.

2. It came in Regulation 4064/89.

3. The purpose of the Regulation was to identify mergers of such a size that they should be controlled by the EU rather than by national authorities which could distort competition.

4. 'Concentrations' meeting certain criteria had to be 'notified' to the Commission within one week of the agreement being concluded, if they had a Community dimension:
   - the undertakings concerned must have a combined world turnover of at least 2,500 million euros; and
   - turnover in at least three Member States is more than 100 million euros, with turnover of at least two undertakings in three states being more than 25 million euros, and combined turnover of at least two undertakings being more than 100 million euros

11.4.3 Reform of procedure under Regulation 139/2004

1. Regulation recognises that national authorities are more effective means of control.

2. The test is whether the concentration creates or enhances a dominant position that would lead to effective competition being substantially impeded.

3. Notification is to national authority unless it would involve notification in three or more Member States then can be to Commission and can lead to one of three decisions:
   - concentration falls within the scope of the Regulation and gives rise to proceedings because it is potentially incompatible with the requirements of a common market; or
   - falls within the scope of the Regulation but there is no need for proceedings because it is compatible with common market; or
   - it falls outside the scope of the Regulation.

4. Art 2(1) requires the Commission to appraise the proposed merger and take account of:
   - the need to maintain and develop effective competition – taking into account the structure of the market and the actual competition;
   - the market position of the undertaking and their economic and financial power as well as available alternatives, access to suppliers and markets, and any legal barriers, as well as the interests of the consumers;
   - even if a concentration of power does not meet thresholds, an EU dimension is possible and there is no breach of Art 102;
   - neither Regulation has seemed to present much of a barrier to mergers – however case law has dealt quite harshly with mergers (*France v Commission C-68/94 and C-30/95 and Airtours plc v Commission T-342/99*).

11.5 Procedural rules

11.5.1 Introduction

1. Powers and procedures were in Regulation 17/62.

2. Now under Regulation 1/2003.

3. The fundamental rule is that infringements of Art 101 and Art 102 are prohibited regardless of any previous rules.

11.5.2 Notification of agreements

1. Under Art 1(1) of the Regulation undertakings themselves must assess whether their agreements breach Art 101 or are exempt under Art 101(3).

2. National authorities can demand that a breach is brought to an end and can order interim measures and also fine.

3. Commission can still investigate and issue Decisions and is still responsible for block exemptions but mainly investigates large price-fixing cartels.

11.5.3 The investigative power of the Commission

1. The Commission can instigate an investigation:
   - either on its own initiative; or
   - on application of Member State or interested parties;
   - it may only take action after an 'appropriate preliminary investigation';
   - and if it decides to act it must notify the applicants.

2. It has extensive power to obtain information from governments, relevant authorities, firms, etc., so it has the right to:
   - examine books and other business records;
   - take copies or extracts from any of these;
   - request on-the-spot oral explanations;
   - enter any premises or transport of the undertaking.

11.5.4 Judicial powers of the Commission

1. Undertakings must be allowed a fair hearing.

2. The Commission arranges hearings, having circulated a 'Statement of Objections' – all parties can respond.

11.5.5 Available penalties

1. The Commission can impose two types of financial penalty:
   - Fines: from 1,000 to 1,000,000 euros, or a larger amount not over 10% of undertaking's previous annual turnover. The amount depends on seriousness and duration of infringement, subject to 1998 Notice on method of setting fines.
   - Periodic payments: incentive led penalties. The penalty is a specific sum for every day or week the infringement continues, so is an incentive to stop quickly. Payments can vary between 50 and 1,000 euros.

11.5.6 Review by the Court of First Instance

1. By Regulation 17/62 Commission decisions are reviewable by court.

2. They will take the form of Art 263 or Art 265 actions.

12

Art 157 and anti-discrimination law

Equal pay:

- By Art 157 'men and women shall receive equal pay for equal work'.
- Art 157 is directly effective (*Defrenne v SABENA*).
- Comparitor need not be in contemporaneous empoyment (*Macarthys v Smith*).
- Wide definition of 'pay' – ordinary basic or minimum wage or salary or any other consideration, whether in cash or in kind, received directly or indirectly – so could include concessionary travel (*Garland v BREL*) and contracted out pension (*Barber v Guardian Royal Assurance Group*) etc.
- Supplemented and explained in Directive 2006/54, which includes an action for work of equal value (*Hayward v Camel Laird Shipbuilders*).
- But can only receive equal pay, even if work shown to be of superior value (*Murphy v An Bord Telecom Eireann*).
- Possible to pay differential pay rates to part-timers provided there is an 'objective justification' (*Bilka-Kaufhaus*) if:

  (i) corresponds to genuine need of enterprise;

  (ii) suitable for obtaining objective pursued by the enterprise;

  (iii) necessary for that purpose.

Equal access:

- Found in Directive 2006/54 – 'in access to employment, including promotion and to vocational training and … working conditions there shall be equal treatment for men and women'.
- Derogation permitted for activities where sex is a determining factor (*Johnston v RUC*) or for protection of women.
- But positive discrimination not allowed (*Kalanke v Frei Hausestadt Bremen*).
- Has been used in pregnancy on dismissal (*Webb v EMO (Air Cargo)*) or employment denied (*Dekker v Stichting*).
- Has been used for unequal retirement ages (*Marshall v Southamton AHA*).
- Usual problems associated with direct effect of directives, but may be indirectly effective under the *Von Colson* principle (*Beets-Proper v F. Van Lanschot Bankiers NV*).

Social security:

- Directive 79/7 extends equal access principle to social security.
- Applies to statutory schemes protecting against sickness, invalidity, old age, accidents at work, occupational diseases, and unemployment.
- Can exclude: deciding pensionable age, benefits for people who have brought up children, wives' derived invalidity or old age benefits, increases granted to dependent wife.

DISCRIMINATION LAW

New developments:

Two directives of 2006 now in force:
- one on race;
- one more general includes, e.g. sexual orientation, disability, religion and belief.

Self-employment

- Found in Directive 86/613.
- Applies to all persons pursuing a gainful activity for their own account.
- Ensures Member States eliminate discrimination.

12.1 Introduction

1. Equality is a fundamental principle of EU law, and is used as one of the general principles of law, so all measures are ultimately subject to it.

2. Sexual equality was seen as a natural extension of the principle of national equality.

3. Art 157, then, was one of the first substantive provisions created to ensure that two distinct objectives are achieved:
   - an economic objective – the elimination of unfair advantages which would distort free competition;
   - a social objective – the general improvement of living and working conditions throughout the EU.

4. Art 157 stated and simply requires that 'Member States shall ensure that … men and women receive equal pay for equal work …'.

5. It was later supplemented by many Directives:
   - 75/117 – the Equal Pay Directive;
   - 76/207 – the Equal Treatment Directive;
   - 79/7 – the Equal Treatment in Social Security Directive;
   - 86/378 – the Equal Treatment in Occupational Pension Schemes Directive;
   - 86/613 – Equal Treatment in Self-employment Directive.

   Now Directive 2006/54, the 'Recast Directive' repeals and replaces all but the last of these.

6. Case law of the ECJ (with the exception of one aspect of *Defrenne v SABENA*) has been consistent in preventing national interests from subverting the general principle:
   - most of the case law in Art 267 references has involved rectifying the narrow interpretations by national courts;
   - it has been instrumental in developing the law on, e.g. fair treatment of pregnant women and other areas.

7. The Commission has also been active, e.g. developing law on sexual harassment – defined in their Code of Practice.

8. Art 157 is directly effective (*Defrenne v SABENA (No 2) 43/75*):
   - It is effective horizontally and vertically because it is a Treaty article and satisfies all of the *Reyner* test.
   - Unfortunately, national demands by the UK and Ireland led to it being only prospectively directly effective.

9. Subsequently, many of the Directives have also been held to be directly effective (but only vertically because Directives fail the *Reyner* test), leading to anomalies and so judicial activism by the ECJ (see *Marshall v Southampton and S.W. Havant AHA* and also *Duke v Reliance GEC*).

12.2 Art 157 and equal pay

12.2.1 The meaning of pay

1. The ECJ has had none of the problems encountered by, for example, English courts in establishing the existence of a comparitor of the opposite sex (*Macarthys v Smith 129/79*).

2. Most actions in the ECJ have focused on the meaning of pay:
   - defined in Art 157 as 'the ordinary basic or minimum wage or salary or any other consideration, whether in cash or in kind, which the worker receives directly or indirectly, in respect of his employment from his employer';
   - so pay has a much broader meaning in Art 157 than in the Equal Pay Act, and interpretation is purposive.

3. Pay has been held to include:
   - perks, e.g. concessionary rail fares for retired railway workers (*Garland v BREL 12/81*) and supplementary payments into an occupational pension scheme (*Worringham and Humphries v Lloyds Bank Ltd 69/80*);
   - bonuses (*Brunnhofer C-381/99*);
   - sick pay (*Rinner-Kuhn v FWW Spezial Gebaudereinigung GmbH and Co. KG 171/88*);
   - paid leave for training (*Arbeiterwehlifahrt der Stadt Berlin v Botel*);
   - contractual non-contributory occupational pension schemes, supplementing state schemes, denied to part-timers (*Bilka-Kaufhaus v Karen Weber von Harz 170/84*);
   - unequal retirement ages (*Marshall v Southampton and South West Hampshire AHA (Teaching) (No 1) 152/84*);
   - redundancy payments (*R v Secretary of State for Employment ex parte Equal Opportunities Commission (1994) (HL)*);
   - EAT has suggested it may include compensation for unfair dismissal (*Mediguard Services Ltd v Thame (1994)*) also – in *Secretary of State for Employment ex parte Seymour-Smith and Perez [1999] ECR 1-623* – the Court of Justice stated that such an award would amount to a form of deferred pay;

- 'contracted out' pension schemes which depend for operation on different retirement ages, as in *Barber v Guardian Royal Assurance Group 262/88*. The case is also important in identifying that Art 157 is infringed if pension rights are deferred in a person made compulsorily redundant to retirement age (if different to person of opposite sex), so applies *Marshall* logic to contracted out schemes, but had prospective direct effect like *Defrenne*.

4. Pension rights are also covered in the subsequent directives, but ECJ rulings are important in UK because death and retirement is not covered by English law in the Equal Pay Act.

5. When considering inequality the ECJ will have regard to every different aspect of pay separately and compare on each level (*Handels-og Kontorfunktionaernes Forbund v Dansk Arbejdsgiverforening for Danfoss 109/88*).

6. This contrasts sharply with the original attitude of the English courts to take a 'whole contract' view (*Hayward v Camel Laird Shipbuilders* (1986)).

7. Contrary to the original UK interpretation of the Equal Pay Act, the ECJ has held that the comparator need not be in contemporaneous employment (*Macarthys v Smith 129/79*) which is now accepted in English law (*Diocese of Hallam Trustees v Connaughten* (1996)).

8. But cannot involve same work but for a different employer *Lawrence and others C-320/00*.

9. It may be possible to pay differential pay rates to part-timers and justify discrimination provided there is an 'objective justification' (*Bilka-Kaufhaus*), which it will be if it:

   - corresponds to a genuine need of the enterprise;
   - is suitable for obtaining the objective pursued by the enterprise;
   - is necessary for that purpose.

12.3 The Equal Pay Directive – 75/117

12.2.2 Equal pay for the same work and for work of equal value

1. Art 119 (now Art 157 TFEU) gave a limited description of pay.

2. Ths was remedied in Directive 75/117 (now replaced by Directive 2006/54, the Recast Directive). This identified that equal pay should

'for same work or for work to which equal value is attributed, the elimination of all discrimination on grounds of sex and regards to all aspects and conditions of remuneration'.

3. 'Same work' does not have to be identical nor need it involve contemporaneous employment (*Macarthys v Smith 129/79*).

4. But discrimination only exists where the differential term is based on sex alone (*Jenkins v Kingsgate Clothing Ltd 96/80*).

5. Discrimination might be direct (*Dekker v Stichting Vormingscentrum Voor Jong Volwassenen C-77/88*) or indirect (*Jenkins v Kingsgate Clothing*), e.g. by giving different rates to part-timers.

6. To bring an 'equal value claim' a woman must show that her job, though different to the man's, is equal in the demands made on her in terms of effort, skill, decision making, etc. and thus of equal value to the employer.

- Proving a claim will depend on the result of a job evaluation study instigated as a result of the claim.
- ECJ guidelines on such schemes are in *Rummler v Dato-Druck GmbH 237/85*. The scheme could be acceptable if:
  (i) the system as a whole precluded discrimination on grounds of sex;
  (ii) the criteria employed were objectively justified, which they would be if:
    a) appropriate to tasks to be carried out; and
    b) correspond with genuine need of undertaking.
- *Danfoss* extended the criteria to include flexibility and seniority.
- Directive 75/117 (now under Directive 2006/54, the Recast Directive) required Member States to ensure that provisions of collective agreements, wage scales, wage agreements, or individual contracts of employment contrary to the principle of equality are invalidated. In *Cadman* (*Case C-17/05*) [2006] the Court of Justice identified that incremental pay scales could be justified on the basis of the extra experience offered by the worker except 'where the worker provides evidence capable of giving rise to serious doubts as to whether recourse to the criterion of length of service is, in the circumstances, appropriate'.
- It is also the Member State's responsibility to ensure that citizens have the means to bring such a claim – so the UK was taken to the ECJ originally under Art 169 (now Art 258 TFEU) infringement proceedings in *Commission v UK 61/81* (leading to the Equal Pay

(Amendment) Act 1983, the first claim being *Hayward v Camel Laird Shipbuilders* (1986)), as was Luxembourg in *Commission v Luxembourg 58/81*.

■ It was shown that provisions in UK law in the Employment Protection Consolidation Act 1978 (now Employment Rights Act 1996) on part-time workers offend EC (now EU) law (*R v Secretary of State for Employment, ex parte Equal Opportunities Commission* (1994)).

■ The old two-year qualifying period for unfair dismissal was also challenged (*R v Secretary of State for Employment, ex parte Seymour-Smith* (1997)).

■ One major anomaly of the 'equal value claim' is that the woman can only receive equal pay, even if her work is shown to be of superior value (*Murphy v An Bord Telecom Eireann 157/86*).

■ In some situations a claim could be brought under the Directive or Art 157, in which case the latter is preferable because of direct effect implications.

12.4 Equal treatment

1. This was introduced under Art 308 rather than Art 119: 'If action by the Community … necessary to attain … one of the objectives … and this Treaty has not provided the necessary powers, the Council shall … take the appropriate measures …'.

2. Directive 2006/54 provides for equal treatment on grounds of sex in pay, conditions of employment, including access to and termination of employment, and in occupational social security systems – this necessarily includes provision against discrimination of transsexuals (*KB v National Health Service Pensions Agency (Case C-117/01)* [2004]).

3. The Directive defines discrimination:
   ■ under Art 2(1)(a) (which deals with sex discrimination) 'direct discrimination' occurs where 'where one person is treated less favourably on grounds of sex than another is, has been or would be treated in a comparable situation';
   ■ under Art 2(1)(b) indirect 'discrimination' occurs where 'an apparently neutral provision, criterion or practice would put persons of one sex at a particular disadvantage compared with persons of the other sex, unless that provision, criterion or practice is objectively justified by a legitimate aim, and the means of achieving that aim are appropriate and necessary';

- under Art 2(1)(d) sexual harrassment occurs 'where any form of unwanted verbal, non-verbal or physical conduct of a sexual nature occurs, with the purpose of efefct or violating the dignity of a person, in particular when creating an intimidating, hostile, degrading, humiliating or offensive environment'.

4. Derogation is permitted under Art 14(2) for 'activities for which the sex of the worker constitutes a genuine and determining occupational requirement, provided that its objective is legitimate and the requirement is proportionate' (*Johnston v Chief Constable of the Royal Ulster Constabulary 222/84*), e.g. specialist army combat units (*Sirdar v Secretary of State for Defence C-273/97*).
   - It is for national courts to determine how national legislation is interpreted, but:
     (i) derogation can only apply to specific duties, not activities in general;
     (ii) the situation must be periodically reviewed to ensure it is still justified;
     (iii) the principle of proportionality must apply;
     (iv) the Recast Directive also introduces a reverse burden of proof;
   - derogation was also possible under the original Equal Treatment Directive for 'provisions concerning the protection of women, particularly as regards pregnancy and maternity …', but the same provision will not protect men (*Hofman v Barmer Ersatzkasse 184/83*);
   - and by Art 157(4) TFEU Member States are able to engage in positive discrimination to prevent unequal treatment of women, this is described in Art 3 of the Directive as adopting measures that allow women to compete on a level playing field, but not to the extent of using quotas (*Kalanke v Frei Hausestadt Bremen C-450/93*).

5. The original ETD also had particular use in pregnancy:
   - where access to employment is denied (*Dekker v Stichting C-177/88*);
   - or on dismissal during maternity leave (*Hertz 179/80*);
   - or for any dismissal purely on the grounds of pregnancy (*Webb v EMO Air Cargo C-2/93*).

6. The Equal Treatment Directive has also been useful in relation to unequal retirement ages (*Marshall* – although retirement ages generally come under Directive 79/7 *Burton v British Railways Board 19/81*).

7. It was also useful in relation to the calculation of pensionable age for redundancy (*Barber v Guardian Royal Exchange C-262/88*).

8. There are the usual problems associated with direct effect of Directives, but may be indirectly effective under the *Von Colson* principle (*Beets-Proper v F. Van Lanschot Bankiers NV 262/84*).

12.4 Directive 79/7 and equal treatment in matters of social security

1. This extended the basic principle in 76/207 (now repealed and replaced by the Recast Directive 2006/54) to social security matters:
   - by Art 2 it applies to the working population: 'self-employed persons, workers and self-employed persons whose activity is interrupted by illness, accident, or involuntary unemployment and persons seeking employment … retired or invalided workers and self-employed persons …';
   - and it has been interpreted broadly (*Drake v Chief Adjudication Officer 150/85* on carers and see also *Richards* (*Case C-423/04* [2006]).

2. Under Art 3 the principles apply to:
   - statutory schemes giving protection against sickness, invalidity, old age, accidents at work, occupational diseases, and unemployment;
   - social assistance in so far as it is intended to supplement or replace the statutory schemes.

3. Under Art 4 there will be no discrimination in:
   - the scope of the schemes and conditions of access to them;
   - obligation to contribute and calculation of contributions;
   - calculation of benefits including cover of benefits;
   - duration of the benefit.

4. So it can apply, for example, to invalidity payment to part-time workers (*Ruzius-Wilbrink v Bestuur van de Bedrifsvereniging voor Overheidsdiensten 102/88*).

5. Art 7 allows Member States to exclude certain matters:
   - determination of pensionable age;
   - benefits for people who have brought up children;
   - wives' derived invalidity or old-age benefits;
   - increases granted to a dependent wife.

6. But some aspects would come under it, e.g. *Marshall*, *Burton* and it would not apply to, for example, exemption from prescription charges based on differential pensionable age (*R v Secretary of State for Health, ex parte Richardson C-137/94*).

12.5 Directive 86/613 and equal treatment in self-employment

1. This extends the principle of equal treatment to self-employment.

2. Art 2 applies to 'all persons pursuing a gainful activity for their own account – including farmers and members of the liberal professions ... and spouses not being employees or partners where they habitually participate in activities of self-employed worker and perform same tasks or ancillary tasks ...'.

3. So, Member States must ensure that all discrimination is eliminated in:
   ■ establishment, equipment, extension or launching of any business (Art 4);
   ■ formation of companies between spouses (Art 5);
   ■ access to social security schemes (Art 6).

12.6 The wider anti-discrimination agenda

1. Art 141 (now Art 157 TFEU) is now a base for introducing directives based on equality.

2. Art 141 was limited to sexual equality, but a separate clause Art 13 allowed the Commission to take appropriate action to combat discrimination based on 'sex, racial or ethnic origin, religion or belief, disability, age, or sexual orientation'.

3. Two new Directives are now in force:
   ■ the first, the Race Directive 2000/43, is on race discrimination in employment (and limited specific non-employment areas) which broadens the UK meaning of indirect discrimination;
   ■ the second, the Framework Directive 2000/78, applies to employment only on discrimination on age, sexual orientation, disability, religion, belief.

4. Both Directives share the principle of equal treatment and the core areas of prohibited discrimination now found in the Recast Directive and referrals have already occurred:
   ■ on age discrimination (*Palacios de la Villa (Case C-411/05* [2007] and *Wolf C-229/08* [2010]);
   ■ on race discrimination (*Feryn (Case C-54/07)* [2008]).
   ■ on sexual orientation *Maruko (Case C-267/06)* [2008]).
   ■ on disability (*Chacón Navas (Case C-13/05)* [2006]).

5. More directives and soft law are due in the Social Policy Agenda.

13

The social dimension

13.1 Art 20 and citizenship

1. TEU laid the foundation is of citizenship – a logical progression of the move away from the purely economic view of free movement – now in Art 20.

2. Arts 21–25 state the individual rights of citizens:
   - to move and reside freely in Member States – Art 21; subject to Member States' rules on nationality (*R v Secretary of State for the Home Department, ex parte Kaur C-192/99*); while it is questionable whether Art 21 is directly effective (*Grzelczyk v Centre Public d'Aide Sociale C-184/99*) it is possible to rely on it in national proceedings (*Zhu and Chen v Secretary of State for the Home Department C-200/02*); and it has been used in respect of migrant students' right to a maintenance loan (*Bidar C-209/03*) or grant (*Morgan v Bezirksregierung Koin and Iris Butcher v Landrat des Breises Duren C-11/06 and C-12/06*), and social security benefits (*Collins C-138/02 and Ioannidis C-258/04*), and the compatibility of national legislation on tax (*Schempp C-403/03*) and employment (*De Cuyper C-406/04*) on Art 21 rights;
   - to vote and stand as a candidate in municipal elections – Art 21(1);
   - to vote in or stand for European Parliament – Art 21(2);
   - to receive diplomatic protection or representation in a state where the citizen's own state is not diplomatically represented – Art 23;
   - to petition the European Parliament or apply to the ombudsman – Art 24.

3. Those derogations found in the Treaty can be applied.

4. However, complete free movement will only be achieved with removal of all border controls – all Member States other than the UK and Eire accepted this principle in the Schengen Agreement.

5. The Amsterdam Treaty integrated policy on free movement, asylum, and immigration – a five-year period was set for implementation, e.g.

of removal of all internal border controls. The ToL provided for the intergration of the Schengen Agreement into the framework of the EU and includes all Member States except UK and Eire.

6. Problems concerning concept of citizenship include:
   - it is symbolic, without real content;
   - the rights and duties involved are not totally clear;
   - it adds little to citizenship of individual states;
   - non-citizens enjoy similar rights in many cases;
   - it misleadingly suggests the concept of a European state which does not yet exist.

7. But the general idea is to promote a sense of connection with the Union as a whole, as well as with Member States.

13.2 Social policy

13.2.1 Background

1. There was no direct mention of social policy in the EC Treaty – policies were originally framed in economic terms.

2. But Arts 136–145 (now Arts 151–161 TFEU) did set out general aims of 'improved working conditions and standard of living' and Art 130d established the European Social Fund (ESF).

3. It is said that the social dimension has consistently been compromised by the overriding economic interest.

4. There was little progress in social policy before the mid-1980s, though the first 'Social Action Programme' 1974 did set out objectives of full and better employment; better living and working conditions; social dialogue in the workplace.

5. With change of personnel, e.g. Mitterand, Delors, a new 'Social Action Programme' was agreed, stressing the need for a 'balanced Europe' and 'social and economic cohesion'.

6. Art 118a and Art 118b were inserted in the Treaty by SEA '86.

7. Followed by 'The Social Dimension of the Internal Market', recommending creation of a Social Charter, accepted by all but rejected out of hand by the UK – resulted in the Social Protocol following Maastricht.

8. ToA was the most important development for social policy, and introduced a new framework, after the UK agreed.

13.2.2 The Social Charter

1. This is implemented through Social Action Programmes.

2. It lays down 13 fundamental principles to achieve:
   - right of free movement for employment;
   - right to fair remuneration;
   - right to employment on same terms as nationals;
   - right to improved living and working conditions;
   - right to social protection in existing national systems, and minimum income for those without employment;
   - right to free association and collective bargaining;
   - right to vocational training;
   - right of men and women to equal treatment in and out of work;
   - rights of workers to information, consultation, and to participation;
   - right to protection of health and safety at work;
   - protection of children and adolescents;
   - guaranteed minimum standard of living for the elderly;
   - improvements in both social and professional integration for the disabled.

13.2.3 Treaty of Amsterdam and the new framework

1. A new Art 136 (now Art 151 TFEU) was inserted, which recognises the Charter and states new objectives: 'promotion of employment, improved living and working conditions, … proper social protection, dialogue between management and labour, development of human resources with a view to lasting high employment and combating of exclusion …'.

2. But it is limited by subsidiarity and economic realism.

3. Art 137 (now Art 152 TFEU), using Qualified Majority Voting, was the method chosen to implement objectives including: improvement of working environment; information and consultation of workers; integration of those excluded from the labour market; equality between men and women.

13.2.4 The European Social Fund

1. The purpose of the fund in Art 162 is to improve employment opportunities for workers and contribute, thereby, to raising the standard of living.

2. It is administered by the Commission.

3. It was originally used very much to combat youth unemployment, but the overriding principle now is to complement forms of aid already emanating from national programmes rather than creating entirely new programmes of aid.

4. Education is, in any case, helped mainly through funding systems such as ERASMUS.

13.3 Protection of workers

1. Apart from free movement and equality there are a number of ways that EU law has sought to protect workers.

2. Commonly these are introduced as Directives through the area of health and safety – Art 151 refers to the promotion and maintenance of improved working conditions.

3. Although the definition of working conditions is deliberately vague, Arts 153–156 refer specifically to employment rights, health and safety, training, social security.

4. General standards have been introduced in legislation including: safety and health of workers at work (Directive 89/391); safety and health of pregnant workers (Directive 92/85); protection of young workers (Directive 94/33); parental leave (Directive 96/34); protection for part-time workers (Directive 97/81); protection for fixed-term workers (Directive 1999/70).

5. Directive 2003/88 (replacing 93/104) (the Working Time Directive) – is a contentious piece of legislation introduced under the old Art 118a – now found in Art 153.

   ■ The Directive lays down minimum standards in organising working time, and so maximum work periods (48 hours per week) and minimum rest periods (11 hours out of 24, and 48 hours in every seven-day period) – different periods apply to young workers.

   ■ It also lays down standards in relation to things such as night work.

- It also provides for minimum paid holidays – four weeks.
- But it also allows for wide derogations.

6. Directive 2001/23, consolidating Directive 98/50 (the Acquired Rights Directive), protects workers when the business they work for is transferred.

   - Incorporated in the UK as Transfer of Undertakings (Protection of Employment) Regulations (TUPE).
   - It basically transfers rights and obligations to the new employer when there is a 'relevant transfer'.
   - The Directive modified and amended Directive 77/187.

7. Directive 98/59 (the Collective Redundancies Directive) applies to those situations where, for example, the whole work force may be made redundant:

   - it provides for proper consultation procedures;
   - and attempts to avoid the redundancy if possible.

8. Directive 80/987 provides state protection for employees of insolvent employers.

13.4 Protection of consumers

1. Before SEA there was little reference in Treaties to consumer protection.

2. Those measures that were introduced had as much to do with protecting free competition as anything else.

3. Prior to this time measures were introduced under the old Art 100 (now Art 115) aiming for harmonisation, including:

   - the Product Liability Directive 85/374:
     - (i) this imposed strict liability on producers for all damage caused by defective products;
     - (ii) 'producer' was defined broadly so as to include anyone in the chain of supply and distribution, including importers;
   - the Misleading Advertising Directive 84/450;
   - the Doorstep Selling Directive 85/577;
   - the Consumer Credit Directive 87/102.

4. SEA, to speed up harmonisation, took to adopting measures under Art 100a, allowing qualified majority voting.

5. Measures introduced by the old Art 100a (now Art 114) were included:

   - the Toy Safety Directive 88/378;

- the Price Indication Directive 88/314;
- the Package Travel Directive 90/314;
- the Unfair Terms in Consumer Contracts Directive 93/13.

6. Following Maastricht and the TEU, consumer protection was accepted as a policy of the EU:
   - to be achieved by internal market measures under Art 114, and specific actions using the co-decision procedure;
   - measures subsequently adopted include the Timeshare Directive 94/47, and the Cross-Border Transfer Directive 97/5.

7. The Treaty of Amsterdam also made a commitment to consumer protection in Art 153 (now Art 169 TFEU), which will be by adopting measures under Art 114, or by adopting measures that support the policies of Member States which include the Distance Selling Directive 97/7, the Timeshare Directive 94/47, the Cross-Border Transfer Directive 97/5 and the Electronic Commerce Directive 2000/31.

13.5 The Charter of Rights

1. Protection of human rights is a general principle of EU law that judges in the ECJ use in interpretation.

2. However, despite many examples of the ECJ referring to the European Convention of Human Rights, and while all Member States are signatories to European Convention, there is no formal link between the EU and the Convention.

3. The EU has developed its own 'Charter of Fundamental Rights', the first draft being produced in July 2000.

4. It was formally considered by heads of state at the Biarritz summit in October 2000, and formally adopted by the European Council at the Nice summit in December 2000.

5. The rights identified in the Charter very much overlap with Convention rights – the right to life, the right to personal liberty, protection of workers' rights, protection from discrimination, protection of personal data, etc.

6. The preamble to the Charter states that it is intended to 'enhance protection of human rights in light of changes in society, social progress, and scientific and technical developments.'

7. The Charter was given legal force in Art 16(1) TEU as amended by ToL:

- however, it does not create fundamental rights that are of general application in national law;
- neither does it extend the application of EU law;
- UK and Poland were concerned that there was no indirect incorporation of the Charter into their own law – so there are no justiciable rights in UK and Poland arising from the Charter except those where the two states have already provided for them in national law.

Table of equivalent numbering in EC Treaty, after ToA, and after ToL in TFEU

EC Treaty	After ToA	After ToL in TFEU
Art 2	Art 2	Art 3 TEU
Art 3	Art 3	Art 3–6
Art 3b	Art 5	Art 8
Art 5	Art 10	Art 4 TEU
Art 6	Art 12	Art 18
Art J.3 TEU	Art 13	Art 19
Art 8	Art 17	Art 20
Art 8a	Art 18	Art 21
Art 8b	Art 19	Art 22
Art 8c	Art 20	Art 23
Art 8d	Art 21	Art 24
Art 9	Art 23	Art 28
Art 12	Art 25	Art 30
Art 28	Art 26	Art 31
Art 29	Art 27	Art 32
Art 30	Art 28	Art 34
Art 34	Art 29	Art 35
Art 36	Art 30	Art 36
Art K.7 TEU	Art 35	Art 41
Art 48	Art 39	Art 45
Art 51	Art 42	Art 48

Art 52	Art 43	Art 49
Art 54	Art 44	Art 50
Art 57	Art 47	Art 53
Art 159	Art 49	Art 56
Art 60	Art 50	Art 57
Art 66	Art 55	Art 62
Art 85	Art 81	Art 101
Art 86	Art 82	Art 102
Art 90	Art 86	Art 106
Art 95	Art 90	Art 110
Art 100	Art 94	Art 115
Art 100a	Art 95	Art 114
Art 117	Art 136	Art 151
Art 118	Art 137	Art 153
Art 118b	Art 139	Art 155
Art 119	Art 141	Art 160
Art 122	Art 145	Art 161
Art 123	Art 146	Art 162
Art 129a	Art 153	Art 169
Art 137	Art 189	Art 14 TEU
Art 142	Art 199	Art 232
Art 145	Art 202	Art 16 TEU
Art 148	Art 205	Art 16 TEU
Art 151	Art 207	Art 240
Art 155	ARt 211	Art 17 TEU
Art 157	Art 213	Art 245
Art 158	Art 214	Art 19 TEU

Art 164	Art 220	Art 19 TEU
Art 169	Art 226	Art 258
Art 173	Art 230	Art 263
Art 175	Art 232	Art 265
Art 176	Art 233	Art 266
Art 177	Art 234	Art 267
Art 188	Art 245	Art 281
Art 189	Art 249	Art 288
Art 198a	Art 263	Art 305
Art 198c	Art 265	Art 307
Art 215	Art 288	Art 340
Art 235	Art 308	Art 352
Art 238	Art 310	Art 354

Index